Sinaloa Stories

Mexican Hillbilly Memories

RUDOLPH CERVANTES

ISBN 979-8-89130-226-6 (paperback)
ISBN 979-8-89130-227-3 (digital)

Christian Faith Publishing
832 Park Avenue
Meadville, PA 16335
www.christianfaithpublishing.com

Printed in the United States of America

CONTENTS

INTRODUCTION

As a youngster and young adult, I, the author, spent a lot of time in Sinaloa, Mexico, with my grandfather. He lived way out in the country in a small village located in a farming community. At that juncture in time, many residents of said community didn't have access to potable water or electricity. The closest phone was three miles away and paved roads were almost nonexistent. There were only two black-and-white television sets in the small community, and my grandpa owned one of them. This was circa 1969. The other one was owned by Machi, the local mom-and-pop grocery store owner.

Every Saturday night at eight, a three-hour boxing card was transmitted from the Arena Coliseo in Mexico City, and Machi's store would be packed with male boxing fans from all over the small village. The fans were comprised mostly of adults of all ages and a few adolescents. That was where I fit in. I was a teenager back then and over time would be one of the (young) adults.

By the time the first six-round bout was over, the small store would be teeming with tobacco smoke, and the entire front entrance would be wide open. Before the main event, there were a couple of more six-rounders, one or two eight-rounders, then the main event, a ten-rounder.

By the time the main event started, Machi would have sold all his soft drinks, his Mexican sweet bread, his candy bars, chips, and a bunch of sandwiches he would have made for the occasion. All his cigarettes would be gone too. Before the actual card kicked off and between rounds, the older adults would talk about current events, politics, the economy, philosophy, and other things. Sooner or later though, the conversation would revolve around the drug trade taking place in the high mountains. There were always a few men present who had firsthand experience in that illegal enterprise.

They would talk freely about their years of experience in that business because they were around family and old friends. Not only that, but they also had family and friends who worked in law enforcement and who would keep them apprised of any impending danger and such.

For years and years, I heard firsthand accounts from individuals who had worked in the high mountains growing opium poppies and marijuana. I heard those stories so many times they were etched into my memory. This book is squarely based on those many firsthand accounts. By the way, some of those men I never saw again because they were either killed or arrested in the high mountains. It's a dangerous business!

CHAPTER 1

Up to High Country or a Sucker
Is Born Every Minute

The following story is based on events that are known to have happened many years ago. What you are about to read occurs all too often in Northwestern Mexico—El Chapo's turf.

Juanito felt like a fool. Omar, his capataz (leadman), had betrayed him. Younger than Juanito by several years, he had been treated like a little brother. Hard working, quiet, and following orders unflinchingly, he had convinced Juanito of his dyed-in-the-wool loyalty.

It all began many months ago in northern Sinaloa. Juanito and Omar had rounded up twenty young men, all of them farm boys from El Valle del Fuerte. Juanito had already done this many times before although this was the first time he had done it with Omar at his side. It did not take long for the young men to get on board because the bait was too tempting. What was the bait?

It was a tall tale about going to the high mountains of Chihuahua and coming back in four or five months with a ton of marijuana and several kilos of raw opium. The municipality of Morelos, Chihuahua, was where they would shortly find themselves taking in the pure air of the Sierra Madre of Northwestern Mexico. Morelos is about 150 miles north of Badiraguato which is from where the infamous Chapo hails.

Nestled among vast pine and oak forests that receive copious amounts of rainfall, the fertile soil of Morelos, as well as that of the whole region, was perfectly suited for illicit agriculture, namely marijuana and opium poppy farming. It was the summer of 1985.

Just a few months before, Rafael Caro Quintero from Badiraguato, Sinaloa, had been arrested by the Mexican government for murdering Kiki Camarena, a DEA agent working undercover in Mexico. Subsequently, all *chutameros* (opium poppy farmers and, by extension, marijuana farmers) began feuding among themselves trying to fill the huge void that Caro Quintero's arrest had left. Juanito would soon have his crew in Morelos, Chihuahua, his home turf.

First, they were driven in a truck by one of Juanito's associates to a little town in the foothills called Choix. From there, they split up into four groups, each group carrying an equal share of the supplies they had brought along and would be taking up to the *Sierra*; some were on the open-air country bus (*la tranvía*), and others hitched rides on big, empty, flatbed trucks headed to the high mountain lumber mills. These supplies would be sorely needed during their several months of backbreaking work which was about to begin.

Juanito beforehand had hired a couple of cowboys to take by horseback the weapons and ammunition that would be necessary for protection and other endeavors such as rustling a steer now and then to feed the "troops." These cowpokes would ride up the Río Fuerte Valley from coastal Sinaloa to Morelos. They would push their gallant steeds over ninety miles through dense, lowland brush forest, absolutely covered with huge, flesh-ripping thorns, then about ten miles from Choix, they would cross the lone, paved highway and go east up the Río Quintana which was a tributary of El Río Fuerte.

Eventually, they would be riding first through a dense oak forest then thick pine woods where water was gushing out everywhere! There were springs, brooks, waterfalls, and ponds, nothing like the ninety miles of desert-like environment they had traversed below. The last sixty miles were idyllic in comparison, a veritable sea of green with very few thorns.

CHAPTER 2

Sabinos, Tortillas, and Tarahumaras

As soon as they crossed the highway (in the wee hours of the morning), they were on the riverbed. For the next forty miles or so, the Río Quintana was extremely wide—about one hundred yards on average. After all, it was the rainy season. Countless narrow tributaries emptied into this river, which was always being pulled to the west, eventually merging with El Río Fuerte whose majestic delta began/ended on the Sea of Cortez/Gulf of California. There is a total of eleven major rivers in Sinaloa alone, making it, along with its prized superrich soil, Mexico's number one farming state.

On both sides of the Río Quintana grew huge sabino trees. These extremely tall, spectacularly wide trees have massive root systems that extend well beyond and even above their trunks. They only grow next to permanently flowing water and are so gargantuan with huge, curving branches that twist, spiral, and turn in every direction that many small critters find little hideouts/lairs within their confines that protect them from predators and afford them *living quarters* (so to speak).

On the other end of the spectrum, these sabinos also provide concealment for dangerous felines (jaguars, pumas, and onzas) that enshroud themselves in the canopy waiting for a sizable four-legged beast, be it a steer, javelina, deer, etc. (and sometimes even two-legged animals—yikes!) to amble on by then, at the right moment, *pounce*! These ambushes quickly culminate with the feline sinking its deadly fangs into the neck of its hapless prey. Many pinecones can be seen floating in the streaming water that brings them down from the vast pine forests ahead.

Once the whole crew was in Morelos, Juanito led them through the majestic pine and oak forest to the "Acevadía." It was an eight-hour hike on winding trails that ended at the five-thousand-foot level (1,524 meters above sea level). The Acevadía was a lovely spot in the wilderness. A full-blooded Native American family—only one—lived there. They were Tarahumaras, a long-distance-running tribe that spoke Spanish as a second language. Born, raised, and forged in the forest, they were as physically tough and hard as nails but very generous and soft-hearted.

For a meager price, Juanito would have access to some of their acreage located well above the Acevadía. What was the meager price? Letting the Tarahumaras consume some of the canned goods, rice, flour, and more that Juanito's crew had laboriously carried on their backs and a little money at the end of this sojourn. It wasn't going to be the first time his crew would have to tote supplies. Every couple of weeks, the "pantry" would get sparse, and some of the guys would have to hike down to the Acevadía to bring back another load—but never more than two weeks' worth. If too much was brought, that would be equivalent to putting a "Free Supply" sign on the hut where they would be living for the next several months.

Some of the local hill folks respected private property and others didn't; it was that cut and dried. As such, the policy that everyone followed was to not trust anyone. Often, the hut would be left alone from dawn till dusk, especially during planting and harvesting, so the habit of bringing only two weeks' worth of supplies to the hut had withstood the test of time.

At any rate, Juanito set aside enough supplies to last for the next couple of weeks, and the Tarahumaras stored away the rest in their spacious "A" frame cabin.

Once the fourteen days of supplies had been packed into gunny sacks and slung over as many shoulders as needed, Juanito and his crew took off. A few guys were also carrying several cartons of eggs. It was a brutal uphill hike, at times almost vertical! They arrived at their destination about forty-five minutes before nightfall, and everybody was completely exhausted. All the guys opted for sleep instead of eating canned sardines. By the time this odyssey was over, very few of the twenty crew members would even want to look at a can of sardines!

Juanito, on the other hand, was as fresh as a cucumber. He wasn't even breathing hard and had carried his fair share of supplies. After all, he had been born and raised in these hills, so to him, it was just a game. As he ate some sardines, he smiled at all the guys laid out on the *tapancos* (beds made out of more or less straight branches set on short, forked poles). Soon everyone was snoring, even Omar, Juanito's capataz (leadman).

Juanito woke up at 3:00 a.m., more than an hour before dawn. He lay on his back gazing upward, taking in the tightly laced palm fronds (the roof) that had been neatly placed, one next to another, each row overlapping the next in a shingle-like fashion, over perfectly straight branches that spanned the length and width of the hut in crisscross style on an "A" frame.

Before turning in, Juanito had lit some candles that were still flickering. They cast a myriad of shadows on the palm frond ceiling, each one taking on different shapes and forms according to the incessant movement of light emanating from these candles that he had placed throughout the Tarahumara-built hut. All this was taking place way out in the wilderness where there was absolutely zero infrastructure. The nearest manifestation of *modern civilization* was a gasoline-operated sawmill and a bulldozed dirt road that led up to it from the coast. That was at least a ten-hour brisk, nonstop hike through a seemingly endless sea of pine and oak that rose, crested and receded, again and again, along this flank of the vast Western Sierra Madre. This flank, beginning at the very distant high ridge, the central point that effectively divides both margins of the range, leeward and windward, ran due west, as far as the eye could see, before disappearing into the horizon and transforming into coastal foothills.

The Tarahumaras used this hut, only seasonally, to pasture their sizeable flock of goats on the surrounding hillsides. All Tarahumaras have goats. They are less difficult to care for than cows and will eat almost any vegetation. Some Tarahumaras will keep a dairy cow or two for milking and one or two bulls for heavy work, but that's the extent of it. Most of the Mexicans, on the other hand, both mestizo and criollo (criollos are people who can trace all their ancestry to Spain, i.e., they have no Native American ancestry), like having lots of steers plus a few dairy cows and a few goats.

Juanito kindled a fire using oak in a big mud-brick oven/stove that the Tarahumaras had skillfully built. He made coffee and a few dozen scrambled eggs then woke everyone up. After all the guys were up, he ordered a couple of them to start warming up a stack of corn tortillas that he had brought along from the Tarahumara's house the day before. The *troops* needed to be well-fed before beginning their long day of arduous labor (i.e., *backbreaking work!*)

After finishing breakfast, the men donned their mandatory footwear: *huaraches de llanta de tres piquetes* (tire-tread sandals with three *piquetes*). This footwear was used by *everyone* living or working in the mountains. You can bet your bottom dollar that even *El Chapo* used to wear these kinds of sandals when he was growing up. The bottom line is that they last, and last, and last!

The only thing that must be replaced, from time to time, is the one leather strap that is used to fasten the tire-tread sandal onto the foot—one strap per sandal. That is what the three *piquetes* (holes) are for. Everyone sipped their coffee while waiting for the sun to cast its first rays of light on the ridge where the hut was located.

CHAPTER 3

Goats, Pickaxes, and Pancho Villa

Right behind the hut was a big corral where the Tarahumaras would keep their goats at night to protect them from the many predatory animals that inhabit the forest. There were obviously no goats there at that moment in time, but those tough little animals had left about a twelve-inch-deep layer of fertilizer within the confines of the enclosure. This stuff put cow manure to shame! It's super concentrated and would be made good use of in the coming weeks.

At first light, Juanito ordered everyone to grab a pickaxe. The land, fifty meters above and fifty meters below the hut, would have to be cleared for *farming*. It was quite steep with a lot of rocks, weeds, and bushes but no trees. This area had been farmed in the recent past, and all trees had been cut down and their roots thoroughly extracted.

Juanito placed all the men at the starting point fifty meters below the hut. Each man was placed at a certain distance from the other in a straight line that spanned the width of the ridge, about seventy or so meters. Once they were placed, Juanito barked an order for everyone to start turning over the soil with their pickaxes and to throw all the chopped vegetation into piles. Although only semiliterate, he considered himself to be an authority on the late Pancho Villa. As such, he would walk among the crew, immersed as they were in their gradual pickaxe-swinging, perspiration-soaked, uphill direction, giving them subjective Pancho Villa history lessons. He really felt that by doing this, it would take their minds off the humongous task at hand. It didn't!

Notwithstanding, they had no choice but to listen to this short, ignorant man who, out there in the wilderness, literally held their lives in his hands. Around midmorning, he ordered them to take a break and drink some water. They gladly obliged. A few minutes later, he chose three of his workers (actually slaves) to carry out other tasks. Two of them would have the challenging responsibility of making sure the two twenty-five-gallon plastic water receptacles (and a couple of smaller ones) would be constantly filled.

The closest creek was about four hundred meters away downhill, an easy walk. Coming back uphill carrying water was another thing altogether. It was brutal. Juanito ordered the third guy to follow him into the hut where he had him clean pinto beans, a lot of pinto beans! Once cleaned, they were put into a big pot. During this time, Juanito kindled a fire in the oven/stove, occasionally peeking out to make sure the troops were back to swinging their pickaxes.

When the fire was finally crackling, Juanito directed his kitchen helper to fill the pot with that pure, sweet creek water and place it over the fire. Next Juanito showed him, step by step, how to make tortillas using Maseca (i.e., prepared ground corn flour). Just add water and knead, and presto change-o, you have masa (dough)!

Afterward, you form as many relatively small balls as possible, then with a rolling pin, each dough ball is flattened, roundly shaped, placed on a heated griddle, and flipped over a few times, then in a few minutes, you have a stack of piping hot, corn tortillas!

When the sun was high in the sky, Juanito ordered everyone to lay down their pickaxes and hustle over to the hut while the tortillas were still hot. It was lunch time! Canned sardines, corn tortillas, and black coffee were on the menu. Pinto beans and corn tortillas were on the dinner menu. After they had wolfed everything down, Juanito ordered the troops back to the frontline. He had only given them thirty minutes to eat. Back to war with the soil, it was! With less than a half hour to go before the sun started to dip below the Western horizon, Juanito barked out that it was time to quit for the day. He ordered everyone to bring their pickaxes with them back to the hut where dinner awaited them.

The days dragged on. Every day merged into the next like a plodding tortoise slowly protruding its head out of a lethargic body then gradually, bit by bit, pulling it back in. Day after day, at dawn's first light, Juanito would send two guys to the creek to start hauling the ever so important precious water which, without the whole operation would flop (side note: water is more precious and important than oil. The future implications on a global scale are mind-boggling!). After seventeen straight days of working from sunup till sundown, the hillside was ready for planting.

Juanito had hidden away a lot of seeds from the previous harvest, and on day 18, the planting began. Every man was given a long, thick six-foot digging stick cut from the vast pine/oak forest which began at the edge of the clearing. Each stick had been sharpened on both ends with machetes. The big boss, Juanito, at the very first light, placed every man at a given position at the very bottom of the clearing, handed each one a bag of seeds, then explained to them what needed to be done.

Every man would be responsible for a three- to four-meter-wide strip of land going all the way to the very top of the clearing. With their digging sticks, they would poke two- to three-inch-deep holes into the ground, spaced about twelve inches apart, drop in a few marijuana seeds into each one, and repeat the process again and again until they got to the top. By sunset, they had finished. That night, under the palm frond roof of the all too familiar hut, Juanito informed them that they had done an excellent job and were well on their way to becoming millionaires! (*Chuckle, chuckle!*)

Without further ado, he chose four individuals to pick up more supplies at the Tarahumara's house. They had gone through their eggs, sardines, and Maseca a week ago and had been eating nothing but beans since then. They were ravenously hungry. All the backbreaking work had made them lean as mean (so to speak) and very, very hungry! The four guys would be leaving at first light so they could be back by noon. This way, the crew could at least look forward to a half-decent dinner. After the last of the beans had been eaten (there would be nothing but coffee for breakfast), Juanito felt like relating more to Pancho Villa's stories.

During the crew's two and a half weeks there, which felt like an eternity to every single one of them, they had been subject to Juanito's worldview almost every evening. It cannot be stressed enough how deeply Juanito almost worshipped Pancho Villa. He would even refer to him as "Mi General!" and would relate to the crew all of Villa's famous battles in sordid detail as if he had been there himself. He also made sure that the guys understood that all prisoners, whether they were allowed to live or not, would have a piece of one of their ears cut out in the shape of a "V," either by Pancho Villa himself or by one of his soldiers. Rumor was that Juanito had killed a lot of perceived enemies and had left the mark of "Villa" on their ears. That was why no one dared interrupt him when he was lecturing them about "his general."

To make things even more interesting, Juanito had taken a guitar with him and sang the troops songs about Pancho Villa's exploits every evening. He had an extremely high-pitched voice which was almost comical (but the troops wouldn't dare ridicule him for fear of inciting his anger). At all times, he holstered a .45 automatic which was always in full view. Juanito was a dyed-in-the-wool mountain man, and that was no joke. He didn't even start wearing tire-tread sandals until he was twelve years old! He used to go barefoot before that. He could walk nonstop in those mountains without eating for three days, just stopping when nature called. He'd drink water, while walking, out of a gourd. He was the real deal! Unfortunately, he did not have an honest bone in his body.

CHAPTER 4

Coffee, Home-Raised Eggs, and Cheese

Juanito woke everyone up well before dawn, as usual. A fire was quickly stoked, the last of the coffee prepared, and at first light, he sent the guys he had chosen the night before to pick up more supplies. He ordered them to have the "Indios" (i.e., the Tarahumaras) fix them a hearty breakfast and to bring back as many of their home-raised eggs as possible. They needed to eat well because they'd be packing a heavy load on the way back to camp from the Acevadia which was uphill all the way. Plus, the trail they would be beating crossed a creek in a few places.

This creek could only be crossed one way: gingerly! Walking over tree trunks that had been arduously and determinedly laid over the rapidly running water at certain points along the narrow creek's curving, deep, winding passage to a far-off river basin was the only way. At this incipient stage of the creek's passage to lower elevations, it had to carve its way through pure granite. That's what made crossing the creek over the logs that had been laid across its narrow span so dangerous! The local yokels had accumulated plenty of narratives going back many, many years about poor souls who had met their end after having lost their balance while crossing and either ended up being broken bags of bones on the granite below or being whisked away in the unforgiving, rushing water and turned into an unrecognizable mass of bloody pulp as the water and jagged granite worked in conjunction almost like a garbage disposal. Suffice it to say that everyone who had suffered that fate had been outsiders.

At any rate, our fearless foursome, after hearing these narratives while eating breakfast at the Acevadia, opted instead for a longer more difficult but safer route. It was on a tightly winding trail that could only be described as one hairpin turn after another that went nearly straight uphill to the same ridge where their camp was located but well above it. Once on the ridge, the same trail wound straight downhill in the same fashion. Once it leveled out, it merged into the same trail that the water bearers used to get from camp to the creek where they drew out that precious liquid so necessary for daily survival.

The Tarahumaras, a very kind, *strong*, and sincere people who had been living in Northwestern Mexico since time immemorial, prudently showed our four burden bearers the starting point of the new route. They told our fearsome foursome it would take them about an hour longer to get back to camp using this route than the one they had used to get to the Acevadia earlier in the morning. So they surmised, it would take them about two and a half hours to arrive, which would put them there before noon. Foremost on our burden bearers' minds was Juanito's order to be back *before* noon. Suffice it to say that they did not make the deadline. It took them more than four hours to get there! Three of our four individuals carried no more than twenty kilos of supplies each while the fourth carried about ten kilos plus several dozen eggs that the Tarahumaras' free-ranging chickens had laid that very morning. The eggs had been carefully arranged in a large woven palm fiber basket. Each layer of eggs was cushioned with goat hair that had been gotten from the sizeable flock of goats that these, as well as *all* Tarahumaras, had. Raising goats was an integral part of Tarahumara culture. These lucky goats were rarely consumed by the Tarahumara. They were used for milking and making cheese, a lot of cheese. Some of the goat milk was drunk as is, but whenever they had the fancy, the Tarahumaras would mix goat's and cow's milk and drink it with pleasure. They would also make cheese using the same mixed milk, and the end product was delectable.

Male goats were now and then sold to their Mexican neighbors who would buy them when they had a hankering for goat birria or barbacoa (both birria and barbacoa are spicy stews). The reason only males were sold was to cull the constantly increasing population since females obviously were preferred. Plus, only a few healthy males would be needed as studs. This was stud paradise for them, as long as they remained virile and at their peak. Once they peaked out and started going downhill, they would be quickly replaced by young studs and, in no time flat, the former stud would be turned into somebody's spicy stew.

Once the Tarahumaras had left them at the new starting point, our fearsome foursome rested a few minutes and had a smoke. Homegrown *macucho* tobacco was bountiful and free for the taking. Dried, tender corn husks were used as rolling paper which meant after everything was said and done, a cigar-sized cigarette would be the final product. It could be relit time and again since no one ever finished the whole thing in one sitting. It would take hours to do such a thing, plus, macucho tobacco has a real mule kick to it. After ten or fifteen minutes, our hearty warriors were now in attack mode.

Hoisting everything on their shoulders with one man carrying the eggs, the guys were ready for the hike—or so they thought. Upward and onward! After about twenty minutes of upward motion, putting behind them one hairpin turn after another, our fearsome foursome were breathing, or rather, sucking in air, like four old mules who were ready for the glue factory. Drenched in perspiration with their lungs screaming in pain and their lower extremities cramped up, all four burden bearers laid down their load and literally abandoned the now shaky safety of their legs. They rendered themselves, instead, to the lovely horizontal position of the ground (with a thud!) like four sides of still-warm slaughtered beef that had been tossed from a meat truck. After a good long while, the four somehow made it to their feet and began moving once again, albeit slowly! About halfway up the hill, they were now regretting that they hadn't gone the other route.

They decided to stoke a fire and warm up some tortillas that the Tarahumaras had kindly given them. They also had given them some scrambled eggs mixed with goat cheese and some refried beans. Yummy! Before they had even finished stoking the fire, the same three Tarahumaras who had left them at the beginning of the trail earlier now reappeared seemingly out of nowhere. Two of them were on mares and the third on a mule. Our guys were pleasantly surprised! The Tarahumaras said that they were concerned about them because they were *greenhorns* and wanted to make sure that they made it to at least the ridge.

The "Indios" put everything the guys had been carrying on the *bestias* (beasts), extinguished the small fire, and led them upward to the ridge. Since one mare and the mule were able to carry all the supplies, Benito, one of the Tarahumaras, led the way riding the other mare bareback. To make things even more amusing, he was stricken with a speech impediment: stuttering! His stuttering was well known far and wide among the regional mountain folk. "G-G-G-G-G-G-Get off the d-d-d-d-d-d-damn horse!" for instance was among many other examples which made the Mexicans chuckle and remark condescendingly.

Meanwhile, back in camp, the "troops" had been working since first light in a nearby dried creek bed. It was now noon, and the fearsome foursome were nowhere to be seen. All the guys were famished! Since yesterday, they had eaten only beans, and the last of them were consumed at dawn. Juanito, who was quite angry with the foursome, took it upon himself to take his thirty-thirty and bring back some meat. He took two guys with him to comb the forest for something, be it a deer, a peccary, a bobcat (which are edible), or even a steer!

Juanito was a prolific rustler and horse thief and downright proud of it. All the local yokels knew he was but were too frightened of him to do anything about it. Outsiders would advise the locals to just back-shoot him because he deserved it. The locals would respond by saying that Juanito was the most dangerous back-shooter around and that no one could ever get the drop on him. When walking in the forest, he always made it a point to stay off the trails whenever possible. He was a bushwhacker par excellence! In any event, in a short while, Juanito had already brought down a steer, a young bull to be exact. Steers were easier pickings, and he had mouths to feed. It was that simple.

He sent back one of the two guys he had taken with him so this individual could bring back another eight "troopers." Juanito's errand boy went straight to the dry creek with the welcome news. There was going to be fresh meat on the table today! He spent no time in selecting eight individuals to take back to the slain steer. The rest were left with Omar, the capataz (foreman), to continue working. The eight guys set off quickly, increasing their pace, seemingly with every stride, until they were trotting, then running!

Their hunger pangs were now propelling them forward in a frenetic, mad dash along this well-worn path that had been beaten out over the centuries by countless footfalls. Their carnivorous nature was now stoked all that much more when they caught a whiff of barbecued beef! They were now flying (so to speak), being hurtled toward the fire that produced that lovely barbecue smoke which filled their nostrils like a magnet pulling iron ore toward its oppositely polarized self.

When they stampeded onto the slain steer site, having salivated more than Pavlov's pooches in anticipation of sinking their chops into some beef, Juanito was waiting for them and had expected no less than the hunger-induced countenance that emanated from their very core. He already had plenty of salted, thinly sliced barbecued beef at the ready and laughingly told them to dig in. With all other thoughts far removed from their minds, they tore into the succulent meat like so many ravenous creatures, each man focusing entirely on his immediate task at hand. Except for extremely serious flesh tearing and chewing, which bordered almost on panic mode, as if someone or something was going to rip the kill out of their hands, everything was silent except for nature's soothing sounds. What a contrast!

Juanito smilingly and patiently waited for them to have their fill and to gradually come out of their hunger-induced stupor. After a good long while, he began ordering them to lend a helping hand in the dressing out of the steer. A sturdy rope was lashed to one of its hind legs, right above the hoof, while the other end was tossed over a thick branch of a massive oak tree right next to where the young bull had been brought down. It took every single one of them to hoist up the steer. Some of them pulled on the rope while the others grabbed the carcass and lifted it up into a vertical position with the head on the lower end and the hind legs on the other. Once the steer was hanging, it was quickly dressed out, and the meat—all of it—including the tongue, lips, jowls, and all the flesh on the outside of the head, and even the brains and milk tripe were carried off. Each man was responsible for an assigned heavy load. Juanito expertly directed the whole operation, drawing on his many years of experience. He had wisely brought along gunny sacks and some plastic containers from camp in anticipation of this moment.

Once back at camp, Juanito ordered all the guys back to work at the dry creek bed except for four who remained with him to continue preparing the meat. He immediately ordered the men to build a huge fire, then he showed them how to thinly slice the meat, salt it, then place it on a big wooden rack that had been built a few days before. When the fire began sputtering, Juanito ordered the guys to carefully set the rack squarely over it. He then arranged more split oak on the fire and over the split oak, plenty of slender, semidry oak branches to produce a lot of smoke. In a short while the meat on the rack was being thoroughly smoldered.

When that batch was done, it was removed and another one was placed on the rack. This was done over and over late into the night until all the meat had been salted and smoked. When the rest of the crew got back to camp at sunset, they began barbecuing ribs and *tripas de leche* (milk tripe). Two of them began making tortillas and grilling tomatoes and jalapeños. In a little while, everybody was feasting.

Throughout this welcome eating binge, Juanito made sure there were at least four guys outside slicing, salting, and smoking the beef. Before midnight, all the work was finished, and everyone was finally snoring on a full belly. At the crack of dawn Juanito, who had already been awake for a good while, woke up all the guys who, by now, knew exactly what the daily routine was.

CHAPTER 5

Barbecued Brains, PVC, and Scorpions

Immediately after breakfast was eaten (barbecued *tripas de leche*, boiled then barbecued brains, over-easy eggs, refried beans, corn tortillas, and coffee with lots of sugar), Juanito led the whole crew, except the water bearers who, a while back, had also been assigned kitchen duty, to the dry creek bed to continue turning over the soil and pulling out weeds. Amapola (opium poppies) would be planted there and just about everyone had more faith in amapola because the *goma* (opium) it produced demanded a much better price than Mary Jane. Plus, it was easier to handle because it occupied less space. One kilo sold for thousands of dollars, *yes dollars* (or the equivalent in pesos)! What must be understood is that the medium of exchange in the high mountains of Northwestern Mexico is not just the peso but the US dollar as well. There are a lot of Benjamins floating around in those hills among the amapola plantations (as well as US bills of lesser denominations).

Amapola likes rocky terrain such as creek beds because this plant uses big rocks to support itself as it matures and grows bigger. A few days earlier, a shipment of flexible PVC had arrived on the country bus which only went as far as San Vicente. That's where the road, which began down below amid *civilization*, ended. Juanito had ordered his plastic piping several days before he had taken the crew to the Sierra. It was going to be delivered to him by some local cowboys who had mules that would be used to carry this more than 150 meters of coiled PVC.

Once the dry creek bed was ready for planting, it would first be well-watered. That's where the PVC came in. Well above the dry section of the creek bed, the water was still flowing, but at a given point, it disappeared into the ground and came out somewhere farther down the creek's winding passage through the majestic hills. A length of PVC was placed next to the flowing water, then under Juanito's supervision, more lengths were attached, one after another, until a hose was laid that went all the way down to the dry area for planting. Next, the whole area was thoroughly watered for the next morning when planting would begin. Amapola isn't planted per se but rather sown.

Early the next morning, Juanito directed Omar to another fertile plot of land that he and the crew would till for amapola sowing. Meanwhile, Juanito would be sowing the tiny amapola seeds which needed to be sown by an experienced person. One needed to measure the direction of the wind (if any was to be had), considering the location and angle of the rocks and the steepness of the land, if any. To successfully sow amapola seed, or any other similar seed for that matter, it was imperative to have a full grasp of all the previously mentioned information plus plenty of experience. If not, the actual plants wouldn't be evenly spaced out over the sown area, and to make things even worse, some of the areas might not even have received enough seeds or no seeds at all.

On the upside, if part of the sown area received too much seed, that area could always be thinned out, but at the same time, that would be a waste of seed and seeds were/are precious. In this case, however, that wasn't even an issue because Juanito was an expert sower. After a few hours, he finished sowing and immediately went to check up on the crew. When he got to where they were tilling, he saw that they were taking a break, so he decided to check out what they had done. "You guys are doing a good job," said he, "but you're going to have to pick up the pace because the sun sets in about four hours, and this area needs to be ready for planting before we leave. I plan to be here first thing in the morning with plenty of seed. It shouldn't take me more than two or three hours to finish. At any rate, let's get to work!"

Everyone quickly got up from their prone positions, grabbed their pickaxes and rakes (the rakes they had honed out of black oak branches), and began working. Juanito was right there alongside them with an oak rake, raking all the weeds and bushes into small piles and then directing the crew members to pick up those small piles and put them in a big pile right in the middle of the plot. Things were going quite well until one of the guys had the unfortunate luck of getting stung by a *vinagrillo*, which is a big jet-black extremely poisonous scorpion. He had bent over and placed his hands under a pile of chopped weeds and bushes when, *zap*, it stung him on the hand! This dangerous creature from hell had been directly under the pile of chopped vegetation. He furiously chopped it to pieces with his pickaxe.

Deep in the wilderness as they were, it was obvious that getting him medical attention was clearly out of the question. He was grimly told by some of the guys nearest to him that unless he wanted to die, they would need to chop off his (left) hand before the poison traveled to his heart. The stung young man adamantly refused.

CHAPTER 6

Scorpion Poison, Thorns, and Government Cessnas

Seized by panic and now surrounded by the whole crew, he began screaming at everyone to step back and keep their hands off him, all the while holding his pickaxe in a menacing position. That was when Juanito appeared, seemingly out of nowhere. He had been on the other side of the tilled area when everything had taken place. He quickly unholstered his pistol and fired a shot in the air to get everyone's attention. He had no idea of what had happened but was quickly apprised. He ordered the young man to lay face down on a flattish boulder with his left arm hanging down. He then used a handkerchief to tie a tourniquet right above his elbow. Then he ordered him to remain completely still and assured him that he would be back in less than five minutes to administer a life-saving procedure.

He took off on a dead run, machete in hand, emanating a determined countenance. In less than five minutes, he was back and not even breathing hard although he had run uphill for nearly a hundred meters. He had brought back several thorns from a huge *maguey* plant. The thorns were about one and a half inches long and were needle-sharp. He ordered a few of the guys to pick up the wounded young man and lay him on the ground face up. Explaining to the frightened young man what he was about to do, he proceeded to roll up the youth's left sleeve so he could begin administering the procedure.

Without hesitation, he began to poke/insert the thorns around the wound, seven in all, until it was encircled. They had been pushed all the way down about an inch and a half from the sting. This was no joke! The poison would be pulled back toward the wound if it had indeed traveled that far. If it hadn't, then it would stay right on the wound. Either way, it would eventually be sucked out. As farfetched as this may sound, this Mexican mountain man remedy absolutely works!

The next morning the young scorpion-stung man was none the worse for wear. He was back among the crew members, working, as if he had not almost lost his life. Once that parcel was weeded, tilled, and planted, Juanito and Omar, Juanito's capataz (foreman), took them to other plots of land where the same process was repeated. Most of the plots were away from water sources which meant that they would be watered by the coming rains. Those plots near a water source were, once again, watered using PVC pipes.

If everything turned out right (i.e., if there was plenty of rain, no insect plagues, and if the soldiers didn't show up and cut down then burn the growing crops), Juanito was on track to harvest a crop which, *at the very least*, would bring him in tens of thousands of dollars. That amount of money among these hillbillies was something for which they would literally kill. Now the windmills of Juanito's mind were attempting to arrive at a very difficult decision.

He was never one who felt comfortable paying protection to the government to be left alone so he could plant, harvest, and sell his merchandise, but that was what he was seriously contemplating at this very moment. But why? This was the first time he had had so many guys working (slaving) for him in a long, long time. Everything was looking good, more than good. If he was able to successfully harvest everything, and even if he had to pay the government 25 percent of his total gross sales (the usual price), he would still come out smelling like a rose. Plus, he really wanted to get out of the business. He had been doing this for many, many years and had only been busted once. He had had no choice but to pay a bribe of several thousand dollars to get out of that mess; otherwise, he would have been looking at ten to fifteen years behind bars, and that just was not going to happen!

Once again, he had been very fortunate all those years to have only been busted once. On the other hand, since he had always refused to pay protection, he had been raided on several occasions. Usually, most of his crops had been burned to the ground. Many times, he had barely escaped the soldiers' bullets/clutches by the skin of his teeth and just didn't feel like taking another risk. Notwithstanding, several times he had successfully harvested his entre crop without paying protection. These instances were not only more profitable, but he had felt exceedingly proud and would flaunt that pride in the many faces he'd eventually encounter who had indeed paid protection. On the other hand, if he did pay protection this time around, the money he'd have left over after paying the 25 percent would be more than enough to open some type of legitimate business.

The last several days, he had seen the usual two-propeller government Cessnas making their rounds way up above to see who was doing what and how much of it. He was seriously contemplating then and there that he would rather pay protection so the government would leave him alone. On the other hand, he knew he could always do otherwise, take a gamble—so to speak, that was always an option.

All the hillbillies knew the government planes did not always see every crop. The planes flew way overhead, and the mountain ranges were huge! Intersected with canyons, creek beds, valleys, and the like, plus the fact that they were absolutely blanketed with dense pine and oak forest made spotting every single *plantation* a near impossibility. So one could take a chance, hoping that his crop hadn't been espied, but that's all it was, a chance.

CHAPTER 7

Caro Quintero, Family Ties, Supplies, and Omar

After everything was said and done, Juanito decided to take that chance. He had taken into consideration that there were more people than ever growing amapola (opium poppies) and marijuana because of the arrest of *Rafael Caro Quintero*, the kingpin of the Sinaloa/Sonora/Chihuahua drug trade at that juncture in time (circa 1985). With Caro Quintero's arrest and the subsequent arrests of many of his head honchos, the breakup of his outfit was inevitable. That left vast mountainous areas free for the taking for anyone who was willing to risk life and limb for an illegal payday. *El Chapo* hadn't come into his own yet. He was still a youngster.

Juanito needed to go down to the coast to check up on his family and bring back more supplies. He and his guys had been in the hills now for a month and were low on everything, so he took off leaving Omar in charge. Besides the sowing was finished so basically the crew just needed to pull weeds, cultivate the soil, and irrigate when necessary. The rains had already started so it was just a matter of days before those seeds sown in drier sections far from a water source would germinate.

Omar was born and basically raised on the coast although his parents were from the mountains of Chihuahua, not far, in fact, from where they were encamped but higher up. From where they were, it would have been roughly a ten-hour uphill hike to get there. Despite being from the coast, Omar had spent a great deal of time in the high mountains when he was growing up. Most of his experiences there were where his parents, grandparents, great-grandparents, and so on had been from. It was the old stomping ground!

He knew how to survive in the high mountain woods. Although not married because he was still quite young, he had enjoyed many trysts with attractive women. He was not like Juanito though. A chauvinistic macho man he was not. He sincerely respected and, of course, loved women. He just hadn't found his soulmate yet. Omar, unlike Juanito, did like to party when he had money in his hands. He could drink for days on end till the money ran out then he'd be back at square one. That usually meant he would have to go back to his parents' farm outside Los Mochis and help his folks with the chores until another opportunity arose that would enable him to go to the high mountains of Chihuahua to farm opium poppies and marijuana—once again!

He liked to converse, laugh, and joke around so he was quite pleased when Juanito left for the coast. It felt like a weight had been lifted off his neck (in fact the whole crew felt likewise). They were quite low on beans and tortillas at this point but still had a couple of weeks' worth of beef jerky left, so things could have been worse. The next day around noon, they received a visit from four local yokels on horseback: two mestizos, a Tarahumara, and a criollo (a criollo is a person who can trace all his ancestry back to Spain, i.e., they have no Native American blood, nor any other non-Spanish ancestry for that matter).

Earlier in the day, Juanito's crew had heard in the distance mul-tiple shotgun and rifle blasts, and now they knew who had been doing the shooting. The four horsemen had been out hunting and had had quite a bit of luck. One of the horses was pulling a travois and neatly piled on it were several wild turkeys, a wild boar, one white-tailed deer—a buck, and several dozen doves. Wow! What a catch! Omar immediately greeted the four hombres and offered them some nice, cool water. He then invited them into the hut to rest for a while in the shade.

They chatted for a bit, the main subject being how the crops were doing, for they, just like every other hillbilly in the area, were also *chutameros*. After a spell, Omar asked the visitors if they would be interested in trading one of the turkeys for some beef jerky. The four visitors did better than that. Explaining that all of them had plenty of beef jerky at home, they asked if they could barbecue a couple of the turkeys there, which would be enough for everyone, and in exchange, they would clean and dress out the rest of the game right there expecting to be helped if needed.

Everyone pitched in on their own accord, and in less than forty-five minutes, all the game was cleaned and dressed! Two of the turkeys were the first to be cleaned and dressed. While the rest of the guys were cleaning and dressing out the other animals/fowl. Omar began preparing the two hapless gobblers that were going to be barbecued. Fortunately, he had located some garlic and a few onions, and there was plenty of salt. Rubbing crushed garlic all over both birds, inside and out, he placed a couple of onions inside each one, tied their bellies shut with some scrap wire, then liberally salted them. He had no pepper.

While he was preparing the turkeys, he had one of the guys build a fire which was now ready for the gobblers. Omar drove two long stakes into the ground, each one on opposite sides of the fire. Both were forked on one end and sharpened to a point on the other. The flames had subsided enough for both birds to be skewered with a long, green, pointed stick then each end set over the forks. Omar stood next to the fire, determined to take care of the barbecuing. He was now heavily perspiring, so he took off his shirt and hat to cool off.

CHAPTER 8

Full Bloods, Mestizos, and Criollos

His thick, straight jet-black hair hung lankly over his copper-colored shoulders. In fact, his whole body was copper colored. As he stood there, standing as straight as an arrow, the midday sun brought out his copper hue to the extent that it shined. He had inherited his mother Leticia's color and features. She was from a Tepehuán mother (the Tepehuánes being first cousins to the Tarahumaras and who live in the Sierra a few days south by horseback) and a Tarahumara father who was a local yokel.

Omar's father was a blond criollo from Morelos who had never been part of his life. After having given birth to Omar, her first child, Leticia soon married a hardworking mestizo gentleman several years older than she. They had several healthy children, all of them being born on the coast—in Sinaloa—except for the first one, a daughter. One year after their marriage, they relocated to the coast where Salvador, Leticia's hubby, had a house already built and paid for. It was just waiting for them.

He was a cattleman, proud owner of over one hundred steers—a small herd, but still, a herd. A couple of weeks before they relocated Salvador, some family members drove his steers down to the coast on horseback. He was back in ten days and wasted no time in putting his affairs in order before their move to the coast. He also had a crop of opium poppies (amapola) and, like many others, (grudgingly) agreed to fork over 25 percent of his gross sales to the government to be left alone.

Finally, the day of their departure was upon them. Leaving his brothers and cousins to take care of his crop and property till he was able to return, Salvador and his family set out on a ten-hour hike to Témoris, accompanied by one of Leticia's cousins, Pablo, who had brought along a pack mule loaded down with belongings, including clothes, that Salvador and family had brought along.

Témoris was a very small town. Rural, open-air buses arrived and left from there during daytime hours. As soon as the sun began setting, all transportation stopped. It would resume at dawn.

They arrived in Témoris about half an hour before sunset, so they just basically unloaded the mule's heavy burden and set it down in an orderly fashion, along with the stuff they had been carrying, right to the side of the open-air rural bus terminal. They were going to sleep under a canopy of stars on a perfectly clear night with a new moon! After collecting some dried horse dung they had found on the road—it was pretty much everywhere—they built a small fire with it to keep cozy. At dawn—or thereabouts—they would catch an open-air bus to Creel, about a four- or five-hour stop-and-go ride. The Chihuahua-Pacifico railroad ran straight through Creel but not before making a stop at its small train station. Salvador and his family were going to catch the train there and take it all the way down to Los Mochis, Sinaloa, on the coast. Salvador and Leticia, over the years, even before they had met, had taken this train to the coast on several occasions.

They satiated their appetite with some fat burritos they had brought along and quenched their thirst at a natural spring about fifty meters from their encampment. Before they indulged though, they made sure to feed the mule some oats they had brought along, right next to the spring. The poor animal seemed more thirsty than hungry by the way it kept drinking and drinking that cool, pure spring water but polished off the oats with ease nonetheless. They felt comfortable and at peace after their burrito feast. The air was crisp and laden with the fragrance of the vast pine forest which surrounded Témoris.

The dawn buses had already been full since late afternoon, so they just kept on their toes trying to snag tickets for the next one leaving with a few empty seats. There were many Tarahumara women who, since the crack of dawn, had been arriving either on muleback, donkey, or foot and setting up shop next to the bus station to peddle their wares. They sold everything from piping hot pinole (ground corn and hot water sweetened with cinnamon and panocha [brown sugar]) to tacos, tamales, other beverages, and fruit. They also had many handmade items such as traditional clothing, huaraches, palm-frond-woven hunting slings, whistles, dolls, toys, you name it.

Since Salvador and his family still had not been able to purchase any tickets yet, they decided to have breakfast: tacos, tamales, and pinole were on the menu. Just as they were finishing their delicious meal, an opportunity arose for them to snag some tickets. Once purchased, Leticia's cousin, Pablo, helped them load their stuff. It was a lot! Once loaded, Pablo jumped on his mule, bid them farewell, and rode off bareback. Shortly after, the open-air bus took off. Salvador, Leticia, and the two children were finally on their way to Creel where they would catch the train to Sinaloa! They happily looked at each other and were nothing but smiles. Leticia told the children to just relax and sleep if they could because they had a long ride ahead of them.

CHAPTER 9

Feathers, Mennonites, and Machine Guns

I t took them *six hours* to get to Creel along the bumpy, ever-curving uphill road. People would get on and off with live chickens, roosters, ducks, geese, and even goats! What a ride! Feathers were flying everywhere amid a cacophony of barnyard sounds! Not only that, these mountain people, especially the Tarahumara, loved to dress colorfully. Bright colors were stretching from one end of the bus to the other. Red, purple, navy blue, orange, pink, yellow, and white delighted everyone's eyes! It was truly a kaleidoscope.

They arrived in Creel just twenty minutes before the train was scheduled to pull out. They wasted no time purchasing tickets, quickly buying some *Mennonite* cheese and bread, and loading up their things. They received a lot of help from their fellow travelers, people they didn't even know but who, nevertheless, lent a helping hand. That is how mountain people are. Once seated, they realized they were quite hungry, so they dug into the Mennonite cheese and bread. Who are the Mennonites?

The Mennonites, a religious group, are originally from Central Europe. Over the decades, they have spread far and wide, from pre-Soviet Russia to Canada, then the USA. They are also found in several regions of Mexico as well as other regions of Latin America. There are approximately one hundred thousand Mennonites in Mexico. They are the descendants of Canadian Mennonites who emigrated to Mexico nearly a century ago, right after the First World War.

The Mennonite belief system is similar to those of other Protestant Christians. They emanated from Northern Europe during the 1500s.

The Mexican Mennonites also peddle their wares (mostly their succulent cheese) at train stations, bus stations, street corners, you name it, and of course from their farms. The women/girls always wear traditional clothing: long handmade dresses and bonnets, and the men overalls or work pants with suspenders, handmade shirts, both short- and long-sleeved, and work boots. Some modern-day Mennonite men will wear Mexican ranch shirts, cowboy boots, and Mexican cowboy hats. Notwithstanding, most men choose to wear traditional clothing including the traditional wide-brimmed hat.

In less than eight hours, Salvador, Leticia, their baby daughter, and Omar were in Los Mochis. The train station in Los Mochis was another animal altogether. There was a heavy military presence there. The train station in Creel had a few soldiers posted there to keep order, and there were even a few on the train, but Los Mochis took the cake. There were soldiers everywhere in green fatigues and helmets carrying huge machine guns. Everyone getting on or off the train was thoroughly screened, patted down (female soldiers frisked the women), and their belongings searched. But why?

In the Sierra, there was always a lot of violence that emanated from the well-known drug trafficking. Although there was violence between the different drug clans, all too often, it was between the clans and the Mexican Army. This violence went back for decades although the government was not overly concerned about the hillbillies fighting each other. It was when the hillbillies attacked and killed soldiers that the government had no choice but to intervene and tighten the screws, which was easier said than done. Unfortunately, for the government that is, the hill folk were always ready and waiting for they absolutely hated the government and all its manifestations/entities. Up in the high mountains, every now and then, some serious battles/firefights would take place with heavy losses on both sides. The media did its best to overlook this situation, which was quite puzzling for a lot of ordinary citizens but for others not so. Notwithstanding, most of the ordinary citizenry kept their mouths shut regarding this matter so as not to step on the wrong toes. Stepping on the wrong toes could literally end up with a person pushing up daisies before his/her time. That's why for the ordinary citizen, his or her motto was, "Live and let live!" The bottom line was, "Don't stick your nose in other people's business!

Salvador, Leticia, little Omar, and his (half) sister, Naya, finally made it through the military checkpoint at the Los Mochis/ Chihuahua-Pacifico Train Station. What an odyssey! They had been thoroughly searched, questioned, scrutinized, processed, and practically rubber-stamped before being given the green light to pass. The whole affair took more than three hours which included waiting for their turn. It could have been worse though. At least they did not have to pay a bribe to get through as others did. Maybe little Omar and tiny Naya pulled on someone's heartstrings. Who knows?

At any rate, they took a taxi to the local rural bus station from where they would board a bus onward to their new home on the outskirts of Los Mochis. They arrived early evening on the very last bus. That was many moons ago.

CHAPTER 10

Wild Turkeys, Acorns, and Spatulas

Every few minutes, Omar would rotate the wild gobblers skewered on the stick over the open fire. The rest of the wild game had been cleaned and dressed (some had been salted) long before the turkeys were thoroughly barbecued. As soon as they were done, everyone tore off a piece and gorged nonstop until the bones were left bare. At this point, the four visitors hoisted their cleaned and dressed game onto their *steeds* and bid everyone *adios*.

Two weeks passed, and there was still no sign of Juanito. A couple of days before, they had gone through the last of the beef jerky and, in their desperation, had even gone to bum some food from the Tarahumaras. Not greedy people, the Tarahumaras generously gave them a few dozen eggs, a couple of kilos of beans, and several dozen handmade tortillas. This only lasted them a couple of days. The Tarahumaras had figured as much.

So early the next day, Benito, his little brother, Joaquín, and their father, Don Jose, paid them a visit. They went there specifically to show them that they were literally surrounded by food and not to worry. What food was that? *Acorns!* Yes, acorns. They arrived before Omar and the crew had taken off to take care of the crops. Omar and crew were at the point where all they needed to do was pull weeds, prop up sagging plants, and cultivate the soil. All the plants were doing well. They were getting bigger, stronger, and more beautiful every day. Our guys had been there for ten weeks, and soon the amapola would be ready for harvesting. They knew Juanito was aware of this which was why they were convinced he would be back well before the harvesting began.

Notwithstanding, the harvesting was still a couple of weeks away, and they needed to eat. That's why these noble, concerned Tarahumara were there. They took Omar and crew downhill in a westerly direction from the ridge which ran north to south. About fifty meters down began a giant oak forest, and there were acorns literally *everywhere*! The Tarahumaras had brought along several empty sacks and began showing the guys which acorns to gather. They needed to gather only the ripe ones. Any acorn that had even a bit of green on it or small, pin-sized holes (which meant it had been infested with bugs), or was cracked, did not pass the quality control test. Since there were millions of acorns, there were plenty to choose from so the quality control test was the least of their worries.

Once all the sacks had been filled, they hiked back up the hill to the ridge and down the other side to the creek. At the creek's edge, they poured the contents of the sacks out onto a big, low, flat rock. Next, the Tarahumaras showed them how to husk the acorns then, spreading them around on the same flat rock, how to grind them into fine meals using big rocks that could be handled with both hands. The next step was to put all the acorn meal into the sacks—an equal amount into every sack—then each sack was tightly tied at the neck with thick string and a length of rope strung through each neck, the end of the rope firmly tied to the neck of the last sack.

The other end of the rope was tied to a sapling at the creek's edge, and the sacks (there were several) were allowed to be taken by the fast-flowing current out into the middle of the creek where they would be pulled back in the late afternoon. During the interim, the bitter tannic acid present in all acorns would be thoroughly leeched from the meal by the fast-flowing water thus making it edible. Late afternoon came, the sacks were pulled out, the acorn meal in each sack tasted/tested for bitterness by the Tarahumaras as well as by Omar, and all the meal was found to be free of tannic acid. Everyone then headed back to camp where the last step—the drying process—was implemented.

An oven/stove, a crackling fire, and a griddle were all that was needed to thoroughly dry the (acorn) meal. Sunlight could also be used, but there were more variables out in the wilderness using sunlight: the meal had to be spread thin over an even surface, and someone had to be constantly guarding it against birds that could not only bomb it from above but could also land on it and fill their bellies. Not only that but also there were also wild animals such as raccoons and squirrels (just to name a few) that could devour most if not all of it.

At any rate, a fire was stoked in the oven/stove, a griddle placed on top, then the painstaking process of drying the acorn meal, a little at a time, began. Just enough meal to thinly cover the (fortunately) big griddle was carefully spread on then, even more carefully, turned over at intervals with a spatula until completely dry. This process was repeated, well into the night, until all the acorn meal had been dried.

CHAPTER 11

Civilized versus Uncivilized, Palm Fronds, and Squirrels

The Tarahumaras had slept right there at camp so they could show the guys in the morning how to prepare the now-dried acorn meal. They were very kind, very civilized, nothing at all how the Mexicans said they were, that they were uncivilized! In fact, it was the Mexicans—especially the light-skinned Mexicans—who very often behaved in an uncivilized manner. At the break of dawn, the Tarahumaras woke up everyone. They had already tossed beforehand more pieces of oak into the oven/stove right on top of the still red-hot embers from the night before.

They then proceeded to show everyone how to use the acorn meal. They made pancakes and gruel and explained to them how to use it as a soup thickener (although they couldn't make soup until they had more supplies). As the Tarahumaras were leaving, they promised to return soon to show them how to make hunting slings out of palm fronds. Omar and the crew ate nothing but (acorn meal) gruel and pancakes the next few days until the Tarahumaras showed up again. The guys were all surprisingly satisfied with the acorn meal. Their hunger was placated, and they felt well. Notwithstanding, it must be understood that, like most Mexicans, they were meat eaters, plus they dearly missed their corn tortillas and beans!

This time just Benito and Joaquín came. "Don" José remained behind. It was incumbent upon him to check their amapola crop because harvesting would begin any day. These Tarahumara also refused to participate in the Mexican government's *protection plan* (also known as "El Control") which meant that they were also potentially at risk. Be that as it may, harvesting was always a joyous time for *all chutameros*. It was also fraught with danger because rival hillbilly clans would raid other crops and, even more menacingly, would steal already harvested *goma* or *mota* if they could find out where it was stashed. In fact, all too often, growers would be kidnapped and beaten until they gave up the location of their stashed harvest. Sometimes, even after giving up their harvest, they would be executed because "dead men tell no tales."

"Stuttering" Benito and Joaquín showed up very early as was their custom. They suggested that Omar and his crew carry out whatever chores they had pending. They would just follow them. Omar did just that. They all hiked toward one of the amapola parcels that needed cultivating and weeding. Halfway there, the clouds came together and burst forth with a lot of thunder and lightning for more than forty minutes. They sought refuge under some pines trees and at first remained quite dry—until the buckets of rain that were trickling down through the branches and needles finally reached them. Then it was all over! The clouds retreated as suddenly as they had come together, and it was sunny again.

They came out from under the pine trees thoroughly soaked to the bone and laughing at each other's comical appearance. They could not have gotten wetter if they had jumped into a deep pool, touched the bottom, and resurfaced. Their clothes were saturated! They took to the beaten path once again and began hoofing it. Once they arrived at the previously mentioned parcel, they immediately gathered a bunch of semidried firewood and located an old pine tree that had fallen down years ago. It was thoroughly covered with pitch. The pitch was literally oozing out of every square inch of it and was impervious to water. They soon had several huge torches lit.

Laying the torches on the ground in an orderly fashion, they began laying the firewood on top of the torches to dry it out. They soon had a giant bonfire going! Once the bonfire had turned into a fierce, huge ball of flames, they chopped down a few saplings and fashioned some racks right next to the fierce flames. They all stripped down to their *calzones* and laid their still-dripping clothes on the racks where they would soon be dry!

In the interim, some Mexican macho man comments were bandied about regarding whom nature had been most kind. This, in turn, led to which one of them could satisfy women more and so on and so forth. Even after they were dressed and working, they were still at it, making wry comments and having a good laugh. This laugh fest continued, slowly dying down, until noon when they had finished pulling weeds and cultivating the soil. They also happily noticed that the amapola bulbs were just a few days away from being fully developed. All the plants had long since given forth a beautiful array of multicolored flowers so characteristic of amapola (opium poppies).

They heated up the acorn meal cakes they had brought for lunch together with some tortillas the Tarahumaras had been carrying in one of their saddlebags. They had also brought some cheese as well for which the guys were extremely thankful. Everyone munched away in silence. The Tarahumaras enjoyed watching them eat, knowing full well that all of them, because of their situation, had very healthy appetites.

After a while, Benito and Joaquín, each with a machete in hand, made their way down to a ravine and soon came back with several palm fronds. At this point, they asked Omar and a couple of the guys to stop working so they could show them how to weave palm fronds into slings. They repeated the process several times until our merry men had a firm handle on it. Once the Tarahumaras were convinced that they *did* have a handle on it, the two brothers took them downhill to an oak grove where they assured them there would be a lot of squirrels and doves ripe for the picking.

With their pockets full of *right-sized* stones that the Tarahumaras had gathered for them, they first watched the "Indios" easily bring down a few squirrels and several doves before attempting to do so themselves. The key was to not only whirl the sling around—that was the easy part—it was releasing the stone(s) at the precise moment so it/they could be launched on the right trajectory toward the unsuspecting prey. In fact, the prey would only remain unsuspecting if the hunters (as they were shown by the Tarahumaras) made absolutely no noise and moved very slowly through the forest, preferably with the sun at their back.

Having the sun at your back when approaching prey, whether they be of the winged sort, the four-legged sort (or even the two-legged sort for that matter) is always the best policy because it gives you a leg up on your target (no pun intended!). The prey's vision is diminished when looking into the sun, and it's that simple. Our guys struck out every single time they tried, which was to be expected because they were beginners. Only practice makes perfect!

They had time on their hands (until the big boss got back) to practice and practice because Omar had kept the crew busy taking care of the many parcels of opium poppies and marijuana plants. They were all weeded, cultivated, and well-watered. The rains had started several weeks ago, and everything was green, green, green! The creek parcels didn't have to be irrigated any longer; the rain took care of that. Those were the parcels, in fact, where the amapola was literally just a few days away from being ready for harvesting. Omar sent one of the guys back to tell the crew to call it a day and go back to camp. He also made sure they were told that they would be dining on squirrels and doves. Whoopee!

Omar, Benito, Joaquín, and the rest would make their way back to camp, hunting along the way. By the time they got back, the rest of the crew had already been there for a while and had been quieting their hunger pangs with acorn gruel. They were overjoyed to see Omar and his companions as they walked into the hut with a bunch of squirrels, doves, and even a few rabbits in their arms. "Dinner has arrived!" gloated Omar (thanks to Benito and Joaquín).

CHAPTER 12

Stuttering Benito, Dance Partners, and Protection

Their joy, however, was short-lived. In the distance, a sharp, mechanical whirring noise was gradually piercing everyone's ears and getting closer by the second. "*¡Es el v-v-v-v-voludo!*" ("It's the he-he-he-helicopter!") shouted/stuttered Benito as he dashed out of the hut with Joaquín and Omar in close tow. For these three, this was nothing new, but for the rest, this was their first time ever, and it was as if they were frozen in time!

Omar instinctively turned his head around and, much to his chagrin, saw them frozen in their tracks *and still in the hut*! Screaming at the top of his lungs he said, "Drop everything, and get your dumb asses into the forest, you knuckleheads!" They instantly woke out of their stupor and, as if a button had been pushed, dashed for the hut's opening 'Three Stooges' style: tripping over each other, pulling each other back to get out first, and for a few brief seconds, immersed in a state of total chaos.

They all finally got out just to see the others disappear into the pine forest about fifty meters away. Sprinting toward that spot, they were relieved to see Omar at the forest's edge waiting for them. The two Tarahumaras were long gone. "Follow me!" ordered Omar. He led them in then went downhill for a couple of minutes until the screaming chopper was almost upon them.

"Everyone choose a tree then do exactly as I do!" shouted Omar to the twenty frightened *future millionaires*. "Everyone grab a pine tree *now*! Make sure the tree is always between you and the chopper. If the chopper is directly above, just hug that tree and don't move a muscle! One last thing, *never ever run*!—unless I tell you to and, in that case, *always* follow me!"

In a few seconds, the helicopter was swooping over that section of forest, going back and forth and at times hovering. It did this for a good five or six minutes as the soldiers on board peered down into the dense pine forest below, high-powered weapons at the ready. At this juncture, the motley crew finally had their wits about them and followed Omar's orders to a T. Everyone was locked onto a tree, moving in synchrony to the helicopter's movements as if the trees were dance partners, and they were tripping the light fantastic in harmony with the whirly bird's overpowering cacophony of metallic clanging.

They hung onto their trees until the whirlybird suddenly sped away in search of greener pastures to be sure. In fact, there were greener pastures everywhere! Some days before, the fearsome foursome, when carrying all those supplies, had been led halfway back to camp by the Tarahumaras, specifically to the ridge above it. From that high point on the ridge, they were able to discern dozens upon dozens of green and multicolored patches, and that was just from their limited vantage point!

Each one was a "medicinal" crop (i.e., marijuana and/or opium poppies), over which the Mexican government's small planes flew intermittently to keep tabs on who was growing what and, more importantly, who had acquiesced to the government's "protection plan" or "control" (25 percent of all gross sales). Those who hadn't acquiesced to *El Control* ran the risk of being visited, from time to time, by military helicopters as our merry men had.

Those surprise visits were no joke. If one had the misfortune of being netted by the soldiers (specifically for not agreeing to government protection), then that wretched soul would be subject to all means of torture—from freezing cold creek baths, with one's head immersed for prolonged periods of time, to being held down while red-hot salsa was forced into one's nasal cavities, all the way to being hung from a tree, feet first, hands securely tied, with a big plastic bag over one's head, taped tightly to the neck.

Drunk, marijuana-smoking soldiers—that's right, drunk, marijuana-smoking soldiers—would get a kick inflicting pain on these poor wretched hillbillies. If said hillbillies died in the process, whether from drowning, suffocation, or just being rifle butted to death, their corpses would be hung in full view as a reminder to all the local yokels and anyone else passing by that it was unwise to not give the government its "fair" share of the drug money. Anyone who did not could potentially face the same fate.

As for those who were tortured and survived, they would be expected to urge their companions to capitulate to government demands. Notwithstanding, even if they did attempt to convince their fellow hillbillies to acquiesce to the government's "protection plan," there was no way they could prove it. That simply meant that if they were caught again, they would be immediately executed, which is why most individuals who survived those brutal, savage beatings left the hills never to return.

Nevertheless, there were always some stubborn hill folks who, despite the severity of the pounding they received, wouldn't even consider leaving the hills. After all, it was their home, and their ancestors were buried there. Plus, they wanted to even the score, which meant killing soldiers, and the more the merrier. The ones who opted to stay were always the youngsters. The older men, if they survived such a savage beating, were not the least bit interested in revenge. They were just grateful to have survived and to live, whatever years they had left, in peace, far away from the mountains—even in poverty.

CHAPTER 13

All Quiet, Bird Gizzards, and AK-47s

Once *el voludo* had sped away, Omar and the crew slowly made their way back, halfway believing that the copter might suddenly show up again. When they got to the forest's edge, they sat down under the protection of the canopy for a good, long while until they were convinced that "all was quiet on the Western Front," so to speak. "Let's go and barbecue some of the game we brought down (thanks to the Tarahumaras)!" said Omar. "I'm sure you are all famished!"

They quickly walked up to the hut and began picking up the wild critters that Benito and Joaquín had handily brought down. They were quite dead but still very warm. The squirrels and rabbits gave off a pungent, wild scent, but the small birds (doves and quails) none. Omar took charge of the skinning and gutting, making sure to set aside the bird gizzards and the mammal hearts and other organs. They might have been very small but salted and roasted were tasty tidbits that titillated the tongue and set the olfactory apparatus into high gear. Plus, there was plenty to be had for all those who valued them!

As some of the guys began stoking a fire a safe distance from the hut, lo and behold, they spotted Juanito, a vaquero on his horse, and a couple of pack mules ambling up the ridge, still a good seventy-five meters away. They quickly advised Omar, who was on the other side of the hut with some of the other men, who were helping him dress out the meat, that the *boss* was back. He quickly rinsed off his hands and started walking down the ridge to meet Juanito and company. There wasn't a cloud in the sky, and it was very warm.

When he got within earshot of them, Juanito didn't even say hi. He just incredulously asked Omar why they were in camp at this time of day instead of working in the parcels. Omar asked him to look at all the *mota* (marijuana) that was surrounding them on all sides. They were standing in the middle of a huge parcel. "I already saw it. It's hard not to when you are standing right in the middle of it. This *mota* is just about ready for harvesting. In fact, we'll start harvesting tomorrow. On the way here, when we were still on the trail in the middle of the forest, we heard *a voludo* flying close by so we got off the trail and ducked into the midst of the trees. I really thought we were gonna find the hut burned to the ground and you guys either long gone or captured. I'm relieved everything is alright," he continued.

"Speaking of harvesting," chimed in Omar, "the amapola is just about ready for harvesting too." Juanito didn't answer him. They just continued walking toward the hut without uttering another word. Everyone explained to Juanito how the Tarahumaras had brought down the game. He remained very quiet. Then he told Omar to have the guys unload the supplies and put everything away while he went to check all the crops.

He asked the vaquero if he could borrow his horse and the vaquero said it was alright if he promised to be back within a couple of hours. Everyone told Juanito to hurry because they were soon going to start barbecuing the meat. He replied that he and the vaquero had been well fed by the Tarahumaras when they had stopped by their home to stash most of the supplies.

Checking his .45 automatic and then re-holstering it, he shouldered an AK-47, got on his horse, and took off at a crisp pace. Back in less than two hours, he looked quite pleased as he rode up to camp. "We start harvesting all the amapola in three days," he calmly stated. "Is there any meat left?" After he had finished eating, he sat in the middle of the hut drinking coffee with all the guys gathered around him.

"Rafael Caro Quintero was sentenced to forty years in federal prison for executing that DEA agent and his pilot," he stated completely undaunted. "Of course, he denies it, but what else could he say? If I had been in his shoes, I certainly would have done the same thing. There's a lot of finger-pointing on both sides of the border, but who cares? Both sides despise us."

Juanito continued vociferating, nonstop, for the next thirty minutes or so. During his diatribe, he related to everyone how Caro Quintero had developed a *huge* operation. He told them that he heard through the grapevine that the *El Búfalo* operation was the biggest one that Caro Quintero had ever developed. He had barns, tractors, and other heavy equipment plus hundreds of workers.

After the DEA agent and his pilot were executed, Caro Quintero was arrested, then the *huge El Búfalo* operation was unceremoniously burned to the ground, and many workers were taken as prisoners. Those who weren't captured escaped into the forest. A lot of people on the Mexican side of the border just did not understand how an operation that big could have gone unnoticed for so long. It was located less than two hundred miles from the US border.

CHAPTER 14

Caro Quintero, El Chapo, and "El Mayo" Zambada

That was way back in 1985 when *El Chapo* was still a tire-tread-sandal-wearing, high-mountain, Sinaloa hillbilly trying to make his mark on the drug trade. (On a side note, in 2013, Rafael Caro Quintero was released from a Mexican federal penitentiary after having served twenty-eight years of his forty-year sentence. The word is that Uncle Sam became outraged and demanded that he be rearrested and put away for life. Unfortunately [for the USA, that is], it was not apprised of his release until forty-eight hours after the fact. By that time, our boy was long gone. Word is that he is living in the high Western Sierra Madre of Chihuahua along with "El Mayo" Zambada and other narco felony fugitives.)

The Western Sierra Madre of Mexico is an extension of the Rocky Mountains. It is vast. The chances of Caro Quintero getting caught up there are slim but not impossible, especially since he has a bounty hanging over his head. (He was apprehended again on July 15, 2022, much to everyone's surprise!) Centuries ago, when the Spanish Crown was engaging in its campaign to subjugate the Indigenous people of Northwestern Mexico, the Tarahumaras, who had been inhabiting the high mountains since time immemorial, just went higher up and further into the endless Sierra every time the Spaniards attempted to entrap them. They were always several steps ahead of the armor-clad, shield-and-sword-bearing, canon-toting Spaniards who could only go so far on horseback with their heavy load, into the mountains. The heavy load, without a doubt, for many of them was like paying penance for past improprieties. What better way to wipe your slate clean before conferring with St. Peter?

It was a bitter conflict between two diametrically opposed mind-sets—the Indigenous people who always yearned for freedom and prosperity with no one breathing down their necks and the long-suffering Spaniards, who took it upon themselves to carry their cross all over the planet (as well as their insatiable lust for gold and silver) and to deem heretics and infidels, all those who refused to capitulate before (what *they* absolutely considered to be) their divinely sanctioned mission. Yikes! Their metal clanging would announce their presence from miles off in the stillness of the mountain vastness where the silence is deafening.

Early the next morning, at the crack of dawn, Juanito woke everyone up military style, barking out orders at the top of his lungs. A fire needed to be stoked in the oven/stove (*la hornilla*), water drawn from the creek, and a hearty breakfast prepared with enough tortillas made to be eaten during lunch. Juanito, surprisingly, had brought some flour so the guys could make flour tortillas.

They were almost in disbelief. Flour tortillas! This was almost too good to be true. Out here in the wilderness, flour tortillas (for our guys at least) were like eating caviar.

A while later, with their bellies full, everyone was drinking coffee, and several guys were smoking *tabaco macucho*. As soon as it was light enough outside to work, Juanito told everyone they had five minutes to finish their coffee and smoke because it was time to get on the stick. Five minutes later, everyone was outside in the middle of the "medicinal" plant patch receiving instructions from Juanito.

"Everyone, observe me closely! We're going to make some "clotheslines," if you will. Juanito then proceeded to show the men how to make simple, but sturdy, "clotheslines" using straight branches. Those that were forked were lopped off on the other end while those that weren't forked were lopped off on both ends. Dozens of holes were then dug in straight lines between the rows of marijuana plants. Next, one forked stick was placed in each hole, lopped side down, then stones and soil were thrown in until each stick was sturdy. Finally, the rest of the branches were placed on the forks in straight lines and securely tied with string. Next, the marijuana plants were carefully yanked out, root and all, and securely tied to the horizontal branches with the roots at the top. This way, all the oil would slowly ooze downward and end up in the buds. That was the theory at least!

Around midday, a government plane was spotted flying over the general vicinity so everyone ducked into the hut for safekeeping. The plane was gone in a few minutes, so they continued working and, by late afternoon, were halfway through. The next day, they were up at the crack of dawn and, after breakfast, were again yanking out plants and hanging them upside down. By late afternoon, they had finished.

CHAPTER 15

Juanito, Omar, and Daily
Surveillance Planes

After dinner, they were "entertained" by Juanito, much to their chagrin. After about an hour of Pancho Villa songs, they were allowed to go to sleep. The next day, the big boss woke everyone up about an hour before the crack of dawn. The workday had begun. Breakfast was prepared and consumed well before dawn's first light, and a hardy lunch was packed.

They divided into two teams, Juanito the leader of one, and Omar the leader of the other. Today was amapola harvesting day, day one of a three- or four-week affair. Both Juanito and Omar would have to teach their guys the proper way to harvest this highly prized "medicinal" plant. Juanito decided it was best for both to take their guys to the biggest two parcels, so they could be there the whole day and not waste time having to hike to other parcels if they finished smaller ones early.

Time was of the essence at this juncture because most, if not all, of the *chutameros* were now harvesting their crops and the government knew that. In fact, the number of daily surveillance planes had measurably increased. Harvesting time was when those who had chosen not to cooperate with the government either made it (partially or completely) or failed. Those who failed wound up disappearing into the forest and then hiking down to the low foothills away from danger. From there, they would catch a bus to the coast. If, on the way down, they were arrested, they would either be beaten to death or, if they survived, be sentenced to hard time in federal prison. Notwithstanding, there were always some who were freed by either family or friends who had agreed to pay a healthy bribe to the government so their loved ones could give it another go the next growing season which was always just around the corner. On the other hand, those who managed to harvest even part of their crop (much less the whole enchilada) stood to gain a lot of money.

Juanito arrived with his crew at the parcel he had chosen and ordered them to rest a while and drink some water. He then proceeded to show them how to harvest amapola (opium poppies). Pulling out a very small square-shaped piece of wood embedded with a tiny fragment of a razor blade, part of it protruding out, he then showed them how to extract the *goma* (opium) from the amapola bulb. It was just a matter of calculating where the sun would be shining on the amapola bulb, beginning early in the morning and throughout the day all the way to near sunset.

The sun's rays would warm up the *goma*/opium inside the bulb so it was just a matter of using the razor blade to make slight incisions on the bulbs where the sun rays would be hitting them. The optimal time of day was midmorning to midafternoon on cloudless days when the sun's rays were at their warmest. The result was a very slight bit of *goma*/opium very slowly flowing out of each incision then stopping when the sun's rays were no longer striking them.

Each bulb was sliced in stages. For instance, slicing midmorning meant scraping the *goma*/opium off the bulb late afternoon and then calculating where the sun would be hitting it at its strongest the very next day. It was then just a matter of making new incisions on that part of the bulb and coming back the next day to collect the resin. This process was repeated until the bulbs no longer gave forth any resin (i.e., were completely dried out).

Both Juanito's crew as well as Omar's learned quickly, and soon all the guys were efficiently slicing bulbs and collecting resin (opium) under the tutelage of Juanito and Omar to be sure. Everyone was constantly on their toes because not only were the surveillance flights increasing, but also, soldiers had been seen on the ground in El Refugio which was only a six-hour hike away. The hillbillies had a very effective, surefire way of communicating with each other when it came to warning their neighbors (friend or foe) of impending danger.

Whenever soldiers were seen on the ground (having either gotten there by helicopter or military transport vehicle), the hillbillies (menfolk only) would disappear into the woods and then immediately send individuals known for their *hoopin'-and-hollerin'* abilities to man certain high points along selected valleys and canyons. Once there, they would start yelling at the top of their lungs that soldiers had been seen on the ground in a certain area(s) and to consider themselves forewarned. Their echo would carry on for miles in every direction which, in turn, would be replicated by other hillbillies on the receiving end and so on and so forth. Sound travels at blinding speed so in just a blink of an eye, everyone for miles and miles around knew what was happening. That's the original way of swift communication. It's nature at its best!

As a matter of fact, even those hillbillies who had acquiesced to government "protection" still had to disappear into the forest because the soldiers would beat up anybody they found just for kicks (no pun intended) and steal any money or valuables their victims might have on them. It goes without saying, though, that all crops under government protection were taboo to all military personnel—except for high-ranking officers. Any soldier caught attempting to steal even a little of any protected crop would be summarily arrested, court-martialed, and sentenced to years in the stockade. This was no laughing matter. Business was business!

On the other hand, all non-protected crops were fair game to any soldier regardless of their rank. It goes without saying that only low-ranking soldiers would fix their sights on said crops and, when given the slightest opportunity, would dive in head over heels to bag as much marijuana and opium as possible.

CHAPTER 16

Military Conscripts, Hidden Bundles, and the Two-Lane Highway

Believe it or not, a lot of young men join the army hoping they will be sent to the high mountains so they can get their "fair share" of merchandise. A good haul could equal thousands of dollars. With that amount of money, one could purchase a lot in a working-class neighborhood and build a small house. With a couple of more good hauls, that small house would be that much bigger, and one last good haul would enable the "soldier" to open a *legal* business. It's done all the time.

Juanito, Omar, and the rest of the guys had good fortune shine upon them over the next ten days. They were able to work from sunup till sundown and, in the process, press the now-dried hanging plants into tied bundles (over a thousand kilos worth!) and scrape more than ten kilos of resin off the amapola plants—an *admirable* haul to be sure! In fact, ten kilos of opium, when processed, would give one kilo of pure heroin!

The bundles were soon hidden away in a cave for safekeeping. Four of the guys, who were armed with high-powered automatic rifles, kept a vigilant eye on all the merchandise 24-7 by living in the cave.

Juanito and Omar always carried around the collected resin on their person. It didn't weigh all that much, plus it was concentrated so it could be concealed. They were still able to scrape and collect more resin on days 9 and 10, then on day 11, all hell broke loose.

At first light, everyone heard that all-too-familiar and unwelcome sound of helicopter blades—a lot of them! Juanito and Omar had already been up for a while making tortillas (believe it or not) and were just about to wake up the guys so they could pack a lunch for another workday, but it just wasn't in the cards.

"Listen! Everyone, grab as much food as you can, the weapons, and your personal effects...*now!* I've got a feeling that this hut is going to be ashes in just a few minutes. Let's go!" ordered Juanito. "Single file!"

All the guys fell in line and ran quickly behind Juanito and Omar then ducked into the forest right behind them. Juanito led them all the way downhill to a creek where there were plenty of sycamore trees and bushes. It was a deep, narrow creek bed that made it virtually impossible for helicopters to get close. So they were safe, in the short term at least.

Juanito told the guys to find a comfortable resting place in the shade and to drink some water. If they were hungry, he said, the tortillas he had brought along were still warm, and he and Omar had managed to snatch up several cans of sardines as they were flying the coop. They could eat that, he continued, along with anything else that they, themselves, might have grabbed as they were sprinting out of the hut. He went on to say that under no circumstances could they build a fire because the smoke would be immediately spotted. Juanito knew what he had to do. He had no choice because he had been through this before.

Yes, he had been through this before on more than a few occasions. Other hillbillies in his place might very well have just ditched these sixteen guys. After all, they were not hill people; they were flatlanders, so who really gave a hoot? In all truth, Juanito really did not give a hoot about these guys either. It's just that he didn't like leaving loose ends. If he ditched them, then more than likely, within twenty-four hours, they all would have either been caught (and possibly executed) by the *federales* (government troops) or hopelessly lost within the vast Sierra Madre which would have been equal to a death sentence.

In any event, he was determined to remove them from the danger zone. This meant leading them on a military-style speed march to the low foothills which would end smack dab on the two-lane highway leading to Los Mochis. It would take Juanito and crew (except for the four *mighty warriors* left guarding the merchandise in the cave) about forty-eight hours to cover the approximately one hundred kilometers to the highway. From there, it was simply a matter of boarding one of the many rural buses that made the route from Los Mochis to Choix and back several times a day.

CHAPTER 17

Equal Sharing, the Quintana River, and Military Patrols

It was late afternoon, and Juanito had just seen Omar off. His immediate concern was now getting these sixteen guys back to Los Mochis with no hitches. By getting them back safely, there would be no questions asked by their loved ones and what he most certainly did not want were prying questions. Prying questions could always possibly be heard by the wrong ears—police ears—and he did not want that, especially since he lived on the coast.

When he saw that everyone was just about finished getting their gear ready and had their weapons cleaned and loaded, he started barking at them. "Alright, guys, listen up! As soon as the sun starts casting its final long rays, I'll make a small fire, just big enough to warm up the last of our tortillas, although there should be enough left over for us to warm up on our two-day hike to the highway, or maybe even further. It all depends on military checkpoints. At any rate, we all need to eat *and equally share* whatever we have here, and I'll also set aside something for the long haul we have ahead of us. This is no joke guys!" Continuing, Juanito said, "We are going to be leaving after it is completely dark. We'll be walking single file down this creek just following the water. It empties into the Quintana River which is going to be our way to the *promised land,* so to speak. I know this whole region like the palm of my hand, so always follow my lead."

Everyone just nodded. They were in a broken semicircle, some sitting on dry sand, others standing, and a few even sitting on large rocks right there in the creek bed where the narrow stream of water flowed right between them, and the rustling of the sycamores formed an idyllic background.

"Any questions? If you do just raise your hands," asked Juanito.

Several guys did raise their hands, and it was always to ask the same two questions: "What should we do if we run into a military patrol, and how many days is it going to take to reach the Choix-Los Mochis highway?"

"Is that it?" queried Pancho Villa's *shoeshine boy.* (It seemed that some of the guys, after tiring of Juanito's endless songs and stories elevating Pancho Villa to Greek God status, had dubbed him Pancho Villa's shoeshine boy. Of course, he never got wind of it!) He told them, shrugging his shoulders, that he could get to the highway in twenty-four hours if he was by himself—but he obviously was not so everything depended on them.

"Hopefully, everything will go smoothly, and everyone will be able to keep up with the pace I'm going to set. It should take us about two days. Incidentally, I know people up and down this river valley. Some like me, some don't. Anyway, if we run out of food, we won't go hungry. Since there are so many of us though, I would not feel right unless I left anybody who helps us a weapon for their trouble. That's all we have to give. As far as the soldiers go, just follow my lead. Getting into a firefight with them is the last thing we want to do. Also, remember this well: *no talking!* We need to keep completely silent because sound carries very far in this environment, and we wouldn't want to be heard by them now, would we?"

CHAPTER 18

Moonlight, Sardines, and Wild Goats

Complete darkness was soon upon them. "Alright, men! Let's get rolling!" ordered Juanito. Everyone had been resting in a prone position for the last few hours, almost dreading this moment, and now it was upon them. Each man hoisted his pack on his shoulders, grabbed his weapon, and fell into a single file with Juanito at the lead. Since it was so dark, Juanito did not want to walk too quickly until the moon appeared, then he would step it up.

Hours and hours went by. During that interim, most of the guys stumbled several times, and a few of them fell flat on their faces. Juanito didn't care though. He kept on striding and expected the guys to do likewise. They had been at it a good six or seven hours when Juanito signaled for them to stop and waved them in closer. Whispering to them, he said they were doing better than expected and that he was proud of them. They were just a few minutes from the Quintana River (El Río Quintana), and once they had walked a couple of kilometers down its ever-slightly-curving but always west-ward-flowing direction, they sought shelter among the countless trees and boulders found on both sides of its ever-widening basin. They (the guys, not Juanito) needed to rest and eat some of the grub they had brought along.

In a short time, they were already making their way down the Quintana River. At the crack of dawn, Juanito suddenly turned away from the river's edge and began hiking up the embankment to a higher elevation. He led the crew into a pine thicket surrounding a big boulder formation. They would hide and rest there for a spell.

He immediately stoked a small, smokeless fire so they could heat up the very last of the tortillas and grill a grip of jalapenos he had brought along. Once the tortillas were warmed up Juanito ordered them to open the last of the canned sardines and begin eating.

Meanwhile, he was going to scout down river and visit some people he knew to hopefully get some food and, more importantly, find out if they had seen any soldiers. When he told them he would probably be gone a few hours, a look of concern appeared on their collective countenance. As he was carefully extinguishing the fire with dirt, he assured them that they would all be alright if they only whispered among themselves or, even better, communicated with gestures. After all, they were still in very dangerous territory. The bottom line, he emphasized, was to *not* make any noise whatsoever, period! He only had to tell them once.

Juanito silently took off, making his way down the river, sound-lessly advancing on the upper side of its southern embankment, less than a stone's throw away from the forest's edge. This way, if any sol-diers were marching upstream or downstream, he could melt into the brush well before he would be seen. They always made a lot of noise, and, in this environment, sound rapidly fanned out a considerable distance, well ahead of its source.

Juanito had the speed, agility, and ruggedness of a wild goat. He never tired and rarely very stumbled or much less fell. He could do stuff in the wild that most people only saw in the movies or on TV. This is no exaggeration! For instance, climbing up and down sheer cliffs carrying a full pack, rifle, machete, and a gourd full of water, and wearing tire-tread sandals was just a game to him! Aside from this, he was also a master hunter and tracker. Survivalist that he was, if he brought down any animal and had no way of making fire (which would have been rare for him), he would eat the raw, bloody meat animal style. He was very extreme, to say the least.

If he was with other hunters, and just to *show off* now and then, he would cut out the liver of an animal he had brought down—be it a deer or peccary, and bite off a chunk of the liver. Then while ripping it apart with his incisors as he vigorously pulled on it with his blood-drenched hands and blood dripping out of his mouth and along his chin, he would give a short sermon between chews and swallows on what a real man had to do to survive in the wilderness. He refused to be outdone by anyone!

In fact, if he was out hunting with others, he would not go back to camp until he had brought down either a deer, a peccary, or a raccoon. Over and above that, if he got back to camp, and someone had already brought down an animal, he would immediately go back out (without resting or eating) and not return until he had killed another one. Once again, he refused to be outdone by anyone!

CHAPTER 19

Palm Roofs, Crispin, and Hot Potatoes

Before long, from his higher elevation point, he espied a small, palm-roofed house down river still a few hundred meters distance. Smoke was coming out of the chimney, so he assumed that someone was there—but not necessarily the owners. It was still early morning.

Before walking up to the house, he remained exactly where he was for a good, long while, just observing. The soldiers were known to sometimes hold people hostage inside their homes, waiting for someone to possibly knock on the door and, in that fashion, waylay the unfortunate passerby(s), relieving them of any possessions they might be carrying. Next, after a thorough beating, they would be expected to inform on anyone they knew who had successfully harvested "medicinal" crops and either had it stashed or had already sold it and were still in high country.

A few days before, the *control* had fallen through, thanks to a foolish new captain, so everyone was fair game. Plus a few soldiers would always remain outside on the perimeter, hidden behind something, just to give them more of a bushwhacking advantage in case any passerby neglected to knock on the door and just kept ambling on.

From his observation point, Juanito was still not convinced that everything was safe. He decided to circle the house from a safe distance, in case any soldiers were lurking about, always staying in the forest, until he got to the other side. Once there he would observe for a while longer.

When he finally got there, he took out a palm leaf sling he had brought along and hurled a rock toward the house hitting it squarely on the side. In less than two shakes of a lamb's tail, a couple of little girls came running out and looked around in every direction for the culprit. Shortly after, a young woman came out with a broom in her hand shouting "Who's there?" That's when Juanito revealed himself.

Still a way off, he shouted back, "Over here!" He shouted again, "Over here!" as he stepped out of the forest's edge waving his arms. He continued walking toward the house while the young woman and the two girls waited out front. At a given point, the young woman said, "That's far enough! What do you want?"

"Does Crispín still live here?" asked Juanito.

"Of course, he does! I'm his wife," she sharply replied, "and these are our daughters. Who are you?"

Juanito politely introduced himself and said he hadn't seen Crispín in years and that the last time he saw him he was still single. She informed him that they had been married for six years and would he please tell her what he wanted. He quickly explained his situation and asked her without mincing words if she had seen any soldiers.

"Three days ago, twelve soldiers came through asking the usual questions. They asked where the men were, and I told them they had gone to the coast a couple of weeks ago, and from there, they were going to go north to try and hop over the border to the USA to find work. The soldiers replied by saying they didn't believe me and that our menfolk were surely hiding in the forest guarding their harvested 'medicinal' crop. I told them I was sorry but that was the truth. Then they searched the place looking for money but came up empty-handed. They said they would be back soon, and that we better have either a lot of money or plenty of merchandise waiting for them. Otherwise, they would burn the place down. This isn't the first time we've been threatened like that, but the fact of the matter is that the men did go down to the coast and won't be back to stay until everything has cooled down."

Juanito believed her. He then asked her (again) if she could spare any food and that they were desperate. She told him they had a lot of homegrown potatoes in a bin out back and to take as many as he wanted because there were plenty. She said she could also give him a few dozen corn tortillas and even a little beef jerky but that was it. Juanito pulled out a thousand-peso bill, gave it to her, then thanked her. In less than five minutes, he was going back upstream, always clinging to the forest.

He figured it would take him between two and three hours to get back to the guys so he was fast stepping because time was of the essence. The soldiers to which Crispín's wife had been referring *might* have been making idle threats, but Juanito couldn't take any chances. He had to assume that they were going to return (although their threat of burning down the house and leaving the women folk and their children homeless had to be a bluff. The *federales usually* respected women and children when it came to the roof over their heads—if nothing else.).

He planned to avoid the riverbank on the way back down until he was convinced they were out of the danger zone—more or less. As soon as he got there, he and the guys would make a beeline south, deep into the forest, then when he felt comfortable, they would start heading west again. It would be a longer but safer journey. Besides, what was the rush?

During his ceaseless striding, the windmills of Juanito's mind began generating troublesome thoughts and even misgivings about Omar. *He, without a doubt, had to have made it to the stash cave,* rationalized Juanito. After all, he knew how to get around in the bush without being seen and was trustworthy. *Nah, no worries, no worries at all,*" thought Juanito. He kept mentally assuring himself but knew in the depths of his hard heart that anything was possible in this business. "If Omar only knew that I've been planning to pluck *all* his feathers this time around. He doesn't though, so it's all good," he kept reassuring himself. About one hundred meters before he got to where the guys were holed up, he thought it best to slowly approach it from different angles. Always keeping a safe distance and staying on higher ground—just in case it wasn't safe, he silently treaded a half circle around their temporary lair.

CHAPTER 20

White Oaks, Black Oaks, and Boulders

Except for the forest's usual sounds, the silence was deafening. That meant that the men were either following his orders to a T, or something had happened. *Should I feel uneasy or not?* he thought. *I'll climb one of these huge oak trees and take a look-see from above,* he assured himself. Stashing the provisions aboveground in the crook of white oak, he gradually made his way down toward the boulder formation. He was constantly stopping, looking, listening, and always crouching.

Forty meters away from the boulders, he began to slowly climb a giant black oak. When he had gotten nearly to the top, he ventured out onto one of its sturdy branches, always staying behind leaf cover, and spotted the men. They were alright!

From his angle, he espied a couple of them standing, having a smoke, and a few others sitting on their haunches. The rest were out of sight. He scampered down the tree and quickly walked toward them then through the pine tree thicket encompassing the boulder formation. He made absolutely no noise. Walking through a narrow but high opening in the boulders, he stopped right where it ended. With his right index finger placed on his lips, he silently walked into the lair. A few of the guys began to greet him, but he held up his left hand and shushed them with his index finger on his lips.

Many of the guys were asleep so they had to be ever so quietly rustled out of their dreams. Waving everyone toward him so they could hear his whisper, he ordered them to get ready to move out at once. A few of the guys began complaining about being hungry, but he quickly shut them up.

"I have some food stashed in the forest. The sooner we leave, the sooner we'll get to it, so let's go!" he strongly whispered. "Everyone, put out your cigarettes—now! I forgot to tell you not to smoke."

"Why can't we smoke?" several of them queried.

"Because smoke carries. If the soldiers happen to be walking by and get a whiff of tobacco smoke, they'll comb this whole area. It's my fault for not telling you though. It completely slipped my mind. Sorry." In a couple of minutes, all the guys were ready. Each one of them had their pack hoisted on their shoulders and their weapons at the ready, just in case. Juanito instructed them to walk out crouching, one at a time, all the way to the black oak he had climbed. Once there, they would lay on the ground, face up, with their eyes peeled and their ears open. Juanito was the last to leave.

When they had all gotten to the black oak, he ordered them to form a single line and to follow him at a trot deep into the forest without talking. They briefly halted at the white oak so Juanito could grab the provisions he had left there. After forty-five minutes, he ordered them to stop at a stream and rest under the sycamore canopy. The guys were winded and drenched in perspiration. Juanito, on the other hand, was breathing normally and barely perspiring. He quickly kindled a small, smokeless fire to warm up the tortillas and some jalapeno peppers the guys hadn't eaten. The potatoes were for later. Some of the guys were almost salivating in anticipation of tasting roasted potatoes. "Why later?" they annoyingly asked him.

"Because soldiers were spotted nearby a few days ago, that's why. Roasted potatoes require a much bigger fire and more time. We can't take any chances, and it's that simple." The doubters nodded in unison.

CHAPTER 21

Beef Jerky, Roasted Potatoes,
and Pushing Up Daisies

Once everything was warmed up, he pulled out the beef jerky much to everyone's surprise. Juanito divided everything evenly. He even allotted himself a portion because he was also indeed quite famished. Corn tortillas, green chili peppers, and beef jerky were not a bad lunch out there in the wilderness. Everyone ate with gusto, drank some creek water, then took a short siesta.

Meanwhile, Juanito climbed an extremely tall sycamore tree to get a gauge on where they had come from and where they were going. Everything seemed calm in all directions. After thirty minutes or so, they were off again, always keeping a southerly course.

They walked for a couple of hours due south then Juanito pivoted to his right and struck a course due west. They kept walking until some of the guys began complaining. They were truly exhausted. Juanito took one look at them and decided it was best to hike down to a creek bottom and make camp. Under the usual thick sycamore foliage, they set up camp on dry sand and took a long drink from the cool, flowing water narrowly threading its way down the creek bed.

Juanito then ordered them to collect big rocks and plenty of firewood. In two hours, the sun would have completely set. Now while its rays were turning orange and getting longer and longer was the right time to kindle a big fire. The guys had roasted potatoes on their minds. They also had plenty of salt coupled with a voracious appetite.

Once they had collected several dozen rocks and plenty of firewood, Juanito ordered them to dig a big pit in the dry sand with their bare hands. After they had dug down a couple of feet, he told them to step back, and he covered the bottom of the pit with the flatter rocks. Then he placed the rest of the rocks on top of each other around the pit's perimeter. The end product was something similar in shape to chimney walls.

The final step was to toss in the gathered firewood and begin the fire. After about an hour or so, there was a thick pile of red-hot embers on the bottom of the pit. They then threw in *all* the potatoes. Now it was just a matter of patiently waiting for them to completely roast.

Every so often, they would rearrange the potatoes turning them over to get an even roast. Pretty soon, the aroma of roasted potatoes was wafting through the air. Darkness was upon them. They were so deep in the forest and far from the river that the possibility of encountering soldiers here, at least after sunset, was slim to none.

Not only that, but they had also already put plenty of distance between themselves and the main "medicinal crop" area. Chihuahua State had been left behind, and they were now in the state of Sinaloa and had, in fact, been here for several hours. In no way, though, could they lower their guard. They were still well within the fringes of *chutama* country.

Before they knew it, the potatoes were done! Juanito told the guys to wipe the saliva off their chops while he removed the spuds, one at a time, from the pit. Using his knife, he would impale each potato and then place it on top of the perimeter rocks to cool down. This was quickly accomplished, but to the famished crew, it seemed like an eternity. Juanito was snickering the whole time. Somehow, in a very perverted way, he was enjoying their suffering. After about ten minutes, he began to dole out the spuds. Everyone got three each—including himself. They just sprinkled on salt and delightfully gorged. He wisely set aside some for their dawn breakfast.

Up at the crack of dawn, they threw the potatoes into the still-smoldering embers to warm them up a bit. After several minutes, they removed them, sprinkled on salt, and broke their fast. Before setting out, some of the guys wanted to pray to *El Santo Niño* (the Christ Child) for protection and forgiveness. They implored his forgiveness for not praying these last few months and, essentially, having forgotten about him.

Juanito stepped aside and just observed. He was a dyed-in-the-wool atheist. As far as he was concerned, when a person breathed their last breath, all they did after that was push up daisies and that was the long and the short of it. In a brief while, they were out of the creek bed and back on their way due west. All the men were following Juanito in single-file fashion. It was still quite dark but gradually getting lighter.

CHAPTER 22

Left Feet, Nonstop Striding, Abstractness

Everyone did their best to try and keep up with the *big boss man* who seemingly never stumbled, lost his balance, or fell. The guys, on the other hand, often looked like they had two left feet. Juanito had told them, in fact, that if anyone got hurt and could not walk, they would be left where they were and sent help as soon as possible.

Continuing, he explained that if this was to happen, he would then advise some of the many people he knew living in the region to go and rescue the injured individual. They would be compensated, said he, with some of the injured person's share of the harvest money. Notwithstanding, he would do his best to get *all* the guys back safe. This way no questions would be asked which, if were not answered satisfactorily, could lead to police involvement.

Juanito kept striding forward hour after hour nonstop. The guys did their best to keep from falling behind. Before they knew it, late morning was upon them! The previous several hours, for all of them, had ceased to exist concretely. Time had now become a completely abstract entity. Distance, space, sound, and spatial relations between objects had all melded together, and they were now living in a vacuum, just trudging forward instinctively.

A disconnect had effectively taken place between themselves and reality. Exhaustion and hunger had formed this surreal state of existence. One by one, they started dropping like flies, and Juanito had not even noticed it. He too had become disconnected from reality but on the opposite end of the spectrum. He was now like a thoughtless machine, pushing ever forward and not looking back. His sole raison d'etre (reason for existing) was to get to the highway.

Suddenly he reflexively reconnected with reality! Spinning around, he stopped dead in his tracks, raised his hands, and was going to bark out, "Halt!" so they could rest for a spell when it hit home that he was by himself. "What the hell!" he shouted in the air. "The weapons! The weapons!"

He ran back toward the guys and saw how they had collapsed, seemingly one after another. They were strewn all along the path they had been treading and looked more dead than alive. His initial reaction was to leave the lot of them. *These weak bastards!* thought he. *They just couldn't take the heat. They wanted to become millionaires but wound up caving in at the last moment!* he continued reasoning with himself.

Of course, it did not matter that all along he had planned to pluck their feathers (as well as Omar's). It was in *his* best interest, though, to make sure they got home safely. He knew for a fact about crooks like him who had once been immersed in similar circumstances, and some of them had to flee the region for fear of being ambushed. Why? Because when the loved ones of the youngsters who went *missing* did not fall hook, line, and sinker for the lies given to them by the crooks then they would either go to the police or take justice into their own hands.

A few of the crooks would attempt to assuage them with money or gifts to keep their mouth shut, and it would sometimes work— sometimes. If that strategy didn't pan out, then they would have no choice but to employ threats to keep them in line. Frequently it worked but not always. When it didn't work, the crooks would usually opt for making themselves scarce. If they hung around for whatever reason, then the cops would wind up plucking *their* feathers (i.e., they would demand a healthy bribe).

CHAPTER 23

Bamboozled, the Montoyas, Lots of Food

I f there was no money coming forth, then it would be off to the slammer. Now and then, some *medicinal-crop-growing* hillbillies of the same clan would pool money to spring their kin. When sprung, then it would be off to the high country for a very long time, sometimes for years, until the heat died down. If they stayed on the coast, then the cops would always be demanding money (and sometimes even harvested merchandise). It was because of these potential complications that it was *always* in the best interest of the bamboozler to get *every* youngster back alive and kicking. Who knows? Maybe in the future, they could be bamboozled again!

Juanito tried his best to determine if he could help them enough so they could get back home. Some were stronger than others. As he walked among them, he immediately noticed that. Those who were stronger responded to his voice, some very light shaking and a bit of water would probably be ready to roll the last twenty miles in four or five days. He figured that the ones who were not responding would be left behind—under his care.

He would do his best to make sure they too were taken care of, out there in the woods, so they could eventually get home. Once they could at least walk with a firm stride, then they would be guided to the highway by another person they could trust.

He told those who had come to their senses that it was incumbent upon him to get some food, a lot of food, and to get back here as quickly as possible. He promised them that he would try to borrow a horse or a mule to get back before sunset. He knew where he was, in a general sense, and where he wanted to go.

Setting his internal compass on the west by northwest, he took off running, not trotting, but running! That would eventually take him to the Quintana River although his target was the Montoya house which was located a few hundred meters from that same river's edge. The Montoyas were old, close family friends. He had known them since he was a small child and was sure he could count on their help.

After more than two hours of nonstop running, he espied the house in the distance from a low-lying hill. It was still a few hours before sunset, and everything looked okay. Fully aware that he had no time to lose, he decided to quietly approach the house from the back.

When he was within hearing range, he stayed perfectly still behind a huge avocado tree and listened. Hearing the murmurs of familiar voices assured him it was quite safe and even brought back childhood memories when those same voices were like a security blanket signifying that everything was peaceful and secure. He walked toward the back with his hat in his hand, entered, and greeted everyone.

The Montoya family had just sat down to have some chocolate and *pan dulce* when they were surprised by Juanito as he walked into their humble, but clean, kitchen. The Montoya family was a far cry from what it used to be many years ago when Juanito's family would occasionally socialize with them. They were never close neighbors—anything but that. The Montoya house was ten hours away, on horseback. Notwithstanding, both fathers had grown up together in Morelos, and that friendship had withstood trials and tribulations over the decades and had always remained intact.

The Montoyas had had ten children, all boys. The only one still alive was Temo who, in fact, lived with them. He had never married. The Montoyas had once been well-known "medicinal crop" farmers but now only engaged in that activity to make ends meet. Their other nine sons had met violent demises engaging in said activity, and there were many other families who had lost sons, even grandsons, in the same fashion as well.

"Juanito!" they clamored in surprising unison as he appeared before them. "What a pleasant surprise! How long has it been?"

"A little over two years. Time sure flies! The last time I was here, this place was full of your grandchildren's laughter. How are they doing? In fact, how are *you* three doing?" he asked, smiling.

"We're all good, thanks be to Jesus," replied Don Antonio, the patriarch. "How about you? But good gosh almighty, please sit down and have some hot chocolate." Juanito gratefully sat down and had a cup of hot chocolate and some sweetbread. He felt the sincerity and warmth of these old friends and, for a while at least, his hard heart softened, and he was able to truly relax. After about fifteen minutes, he began explaining to them why he was there without cutting any frills. He spoke with complete frankness and candor.

As he fully expected, they told him not to fret. He could count on their complete and unhindered support. Doña (Donia) Lola, Don Antonio's wife, immediately marched to the kitchen and began preparing a lot of food for the guys—for food they had in abundance. Temo went to ready the animals—a mare and a mule. Meanwhile, Juanito and Don Antonio discussed the situation and how to best successfully resolve it.

In one hour, Doña (Donia) Lola had prepared three days' worth of vittles for the stricken men. There would be more coming as warranted. Temo would accompany Juanito to the spot where the men lay and help him nurse them back to full strength. In three days, he would return home to pick up more food as needed. He would also guide those men who were the first to regain their strength to the highway.

During their conversation, Don Antonio told Juanito they had not seen any soldiers on the ground in over a week. Notwithstanding, they had seen military helicopters buzzing through almost daily. On a positive note, there were no major medicinal crops planted nearby which, more than likely, is why the choppers never landed in proximity.

Be that as it may, Juanito and Temo were soon on their *steeds*, all loaded up and riding at a crisp pace toward the *spot* They arrived about twenty minutes before the sun disappeared over the horizon. A small fire was immediately stoked right in the middle of where the *future millionaires* were still lying in a completely prone position. Our two caretakers placed the exhausted men in a circle around the fire. Some were able to hobble over while leaning on either Juanito or Temo, and several had to be literally carried.

They were still in bad shape, but after slowly ingesting some good home-cooked food, they began to feel much better. Juanito even made them some coffee and then let the fire die down. He had reluctantly made it just to warm up the tortillas and prepare the coffee. Plus, he knew beforehand that a fire would psychologically comfort them although it was taking a small gamble. Notwithstanding, he was 99 percent sure that they were far enough from the main military converging area so as not to be seen.

CHAPTER 24

Back in the Cave

Omar had been asked by the four guys if he knew about Juanito's intentions. He felt like he was on a slippery slope. They related to him that a person they had crossed paths with on their way back from the Tarahumara's house had told them to be extremely careful with Juanito. He was well known for bringing up flatlanders to the high mountains with promises of big money only to end up hoodwinking them. After everything was harvested, he would leave them high and dry by telling them that the merchandise had been stolen.

Omar knew about this but did not dare let on to the guys that he had known all along. Otherwise, he could find himself on the hot seat—or maybe even worse.

This time around though, he had a hunch he would also be left out in the cold by the *big boss man*. He told the guys about an encounter he had had with Manuel Adriano the night before at the Tarahumaras' home and how he had been told the same thing. Furthermore, Adriano assured him, over and above that, how Juanito was a dead man walking. The question was, then what should he and the guys do?

"Any suggestions?" queried Omar. All four guys just shook their heads.

After a few seconds, one of them declared, "I, for one, sure as hell didn't come all the way to the Sierra just to go back empty-handed after all these months." The rest nodded in agreement. Gazing at the ground, arms crossed, Omar was apparently in deep thought. He then gazed up, taking in the contours, fissures, and other features of the cave's ceiling, or seemingly so.

After a brief interim, he took a deep breath, shrugged his shoulders, and said, "Everybody, come near and listen." All four of them moved in closer.

"We all want to get compensated for the extremely hard work we have invested here over these last several months, right? We are workers, *proletariats*, and we certainly are not going to let ourselves be hoodwinked out of our hard-earned money by some barbaric *lumpenproletariat* who sides with the *capitalists*!" Everyone nodded in agreement even though they did not understand all the words. "So we all unanimously agree that Juanito is going to try and swindle us out of our just share of the merchandise, right?" The men loudly murmured among themselves, uttering anything and everything about Juanito except for niceties or even the remotest shred of respect. He was the enemy.

Now where in blazes did a country boy like Omar acquire such important-sounding terms? In school! Yes, in school! What must be understood is that Mexico's government schools, since at least the 1930s, have formally incorporated Marxist-Leninist concepts into their curriculum. In fact, elementary school, up to and including the fifth grade, has been mandatory in Mexico for at least seventy-five years. This, of course, has always been contingent on the extension and availability of infrastructure, textbooks, etc.

Marxist-Leninist concepts, notwithstanding, have been, or at least used to be, more frequently espoused at the secondary level. At the autonomous university level, they were once thought to be the panacea for *all* socioeconomic-political ills.

In the late 1970s/early 1980s, there was a national backlash against these teachings. This backlash was led and fostered by members of Mexico's elite, well-established ruling class. This ruling class was anti-PRI (Institutional Revolutionary Party), pro-capitalist, and as such, supporters of pro-Western interests.

CHAPTER 25

Neoliberalism, Third-Grade Education, Government Protection

Beginning in the late 1980s and lasting for the next thirty or so years (up until December 1, 2018, to be exact), Mexico was ruled by presidents who believed in *neoliberalism*. Carlos Salinas de Gortari's presidency (1988–1994) began selling off to the highest bidders, both domestic and foreign, Mexico's national resources beginning with its vast oil reserves.

It wanted to counter Marxist-Leninist concepts because it was felt that these concepts had poisoned the collective mindset of Mexico over the previous several decades. As strange as it seems, both Salinas de Gortari as well as the next president, Ernesto Zedillo, were both longtime members of, and firmly entrenched in, the PRI. Their interpretation of PRI doctrine differed, to say the least, from that of the collectivity and caused a lot of headbutting.

Hard-core Marxist-Leninists do not die easily though. They are still very much around with their dyed-in-the-wool concepts and are seemingly going nowhere with their fossilized world view. They still believe, or at least give lip service, to the belief that the *dictatorship of the proletariat* will one day reign supreme. Not surprisingly, they view capitalism as fossilized and about to turn to dust, thus heralding in a *new era* which, in time, will usher in an earthly paradise (yeah right!).

Believe it or not, there are more than a few university scholars who believe and teach that capitalism and Marxism/communism are opposite halves of the same coin. Wow! In any event, since Omar had gone all the way through middle school, his worldview had been influenced by communist terms such as *proletariat, lumpen, comrade,* and others. Notwithstanding, like most Mexicans bereft of higher education, he lacked a deep understanding of said concepts.

Omar's four colleagues had only gotten as far as the third grade because their respective families had pulled them out of school to help on their farms. So essentially, they were completely ignorant of these concepts. However, all four of them looked up to Omar because he had finished middle school. In their eyes, whatever he thought should be done was fine with them—as long as they got paid.

Omar made it exceedingly clear to them that Juanito would be furious, insulted, and bloodthirsty when he realized that *he* had been bamboozled and not the other way around. He also made them understand that he (Omar) would be the main target of Juanito's fury, not them. Notwithstanding, it would be incumbent for all of them to stay on their toes and never drop their guard for years to come.

While they were in the middle of all this palavering, they heard a couple of whirlybirds buzz on by. Yikes! That close! They all lowered their voices to whispers out of sheer caution. After a couple of minutes, Omar surmised that the *federales* (the military) would not be there that much longer.

Since the *control* had fallen through because of the new captain's ignorance, all the hillbilly men had fled into the forest. Those who had acquiesced to government "protection," or otherwise, were nowhere to be seen. In fact, those who had already harvested most, if not all, of their crops were already on the coast or well on their way.

Those who had not begun to harvest had no choice but to stick around hoping things would calm down. They were all aware that the new captain would eventually have to come to his senses or more than likely be brought to his senses by his superiors. With no money coming in from the area to which he had been assigned, their coffers were now quite low, and they were absolutely incensed.

Sure enough, after three days, the new captain announced (through the grapevine) that he had arrived at a new agreement with a couple of mountain men representing the interests of the collectivity. He, the new captain, now understood that he had made a grave mistake and was attempting to rectify everything. Too little too late. The kickbacks the government had expected to take in were going to be reduced to about one-third because so many "medicinal crop" farmers had just up and left leaving their marijuana harvest under armed guard (which was in no way a guarantee). They carried their *goma* on their person so they could just sell it on the coast if they seriously needed cash.

Omar found this out when he snuck over to the Tarahumara's house to see if he could garner some information about the local scene. He was stoked. Now all he had to do was send word to the pair of local yokels who were now the mediators between the growers and the government advising them that he wanted government protection. Because of the unusual circumstances, he would get even better than that.

CHAPTER 26

Smiles, Handshaking, Cooperation

There were fifty or more soldiers encamped in San Vicente, the little village where Juanito, Omar, and the crew had originally arrived months ago. There were a couple of *voludos* and a few military trucks parked alongside them. They had made it exceedingly clear to everyone in San Vicente that their presence was nonthreatening. In fact, they wanted to cooperate.

Great balls of fire did they ever want to cooperate! The closest fort was in Choix, Sinaloa, and our young captain had been ordered to report there at once. He was ordered to get back into the good graces of the local hill folk, and this was no joke!

Because of his oppositional behavior and obsessive compulsiveness, the flow of money to the high-ranking officers in Choix had come to a screeching halt. They were furious! Vacations had been planned, new cars were going to be bought, expensive clothes for wives and girlfriends had already been promised, and now this.

The young captain had only been gone for less than forty-right hours when he returned to San Vicente a changed man. He had seemingly experienced an epiphany! He was all smiles upon smiles and shaking calloused hillbilly hand after hillbilly hand nonstop. A group of local yokels hidden in the woods had heard about this sudden and unexpected behavior but still were not convinced. They pulled straws to decide who would go and confer with the new captain. Three of them were chosen, employing this nonemotional, "scientific" method.

The hidden hillbillies had been told through the *hoopin'-and-hollerin'* hillbilly grapevine that the now-*reborn* captain would be in San Vicente's esplanade, listening and working everything out with the farmers. The three chosen men showed up and were given a warm greeting and even offered food and drink. They politely refused the vittles and instead asked the captain what was on his mind.

With a big smile on his face, he asked them to please sit down and get comfortable. On the contrary, he wanted to know what was on *their* minds and to speak with complete frankness. They did and were in complete disbelief when he offered to buy all their merchandise at top dollar. The new captain immediately noticed their bewilderment and offered them cash on the line—on the line! But it got even better than that.

He said he would consign them the money and then wait for them to bring back the merchandise. If it was too much to transport in one fell swoop, he offered them helicopters (as a medium of transport, that is). Our three unsung heroes replied that they would first have to consult with their associates before accepting any offers. Word would be sent back within twenty-four hours.

The captain completely understood. In so many words, he told them that his cup overrunneth with patience and not to fret. Patience was a virtue, he said, and everything was going to be as "right as rain" (was this the same guy?). Our three emissaries politely excused themselves and then disappeared into the forest.

CHAPTER 27

A New Control, Brisk Business, Counting the Loot

During this interim Omar had attempted to get word to Manuel Adriano about his wanting to contact the two new "intermediaries" (i.e., the two hillbillies who were now the liaisons for the remaining "medicinal crop" farmers). They, in essence, represented their interests concerning the new *control* of the government. He had told the Tarahumaras he would be back in three days to see if they had any information for him. Three days later he was back.

The Tarahumaras happily told him that the new *control* was in place and working out well. Both sides were pleased, and business was brisk taking into consideration what had happened. They told him he could just go directly to the esplanade in San Vicente to negotiate with the formerly sadistic captain. All the local hill folks were thoroughly convinced the government wanted to make amends. In fact, it was bending over backward to please all the farmers.

When Omar arrived at the esplanade, he observed the three gentlemen who had drawn straws a few days before walking away from the captain. They had just turned in their harvest and had received a military escort from deep within the forest, from an undisclosed location. Why the escort? They didn't want to be waylaid on the way to the esplanade by hillbilly bushwhackers. Seven horses and three mules were what they needed to transport their harvest. Each mule hauled a travois laden with merchandise plus whatever could fit on its back.

When Omar was updated about how things had changed, he had absolutely no problem speaking with the captain. He opted for being consigned the money just as the three straw-picking hillbillies did. He took the money and asked to be taken by helicopter to the stash cave so the merchandise could be loaded, although it would probably take a couple of trips.

He directed the pilot to land in a clearing about one hundred meters from the slope where the cave was located. Once out, he told them to be back the next day at noon so they could start loading up all the merchandise. The pilot and two soldiers with him took off smiling and waving. Omar was extremely excited. This was his first helicopter ride ever!

As they sped away, Omar, in turn, waved and smiled. Once they were out of sight, he ran all the way to the slope feeling more comfortable when he was amid the forest at the slope's foot. He took out the loot, recounted it, then climbed up to the cave. The guys were excited, to say the least. When they had heard the chopper so close, they did not know what to think so they crept between the huge boulders at the cave's entrance to observe. Seeing it land, they fully expected a bunch of soldiers to pour out. Then when they saw Omar exit waving goodbye, they knew at that precise moment everything was alright.

Omar related to them what was going to happen at noon tomorrow. All four of them raised their brows in disbelief. "Are you crazy? You mean you are going to trust these guys? In case you have forgotten, they are soldiers, remember? *They are soldiers!*

With a smile on his face and a big chuckle, Omar pulled out a huge wad of cash. The guys were taken aback.

"Where did that come from?" they vigorously queried, almost demanding to know.

"I got it from the captain who came here spitting fire. Do you remember him?"

"Of course, we do!" They answered in unison. "Do you mean that the government is buying this stuff now?" they exasperatingly asked.

Omar then explained that no one was exactly sure how things were working out except the government. The original buyers had been scared off from this area (just like most growers) which meant that they most likely went off to another region of the Sierra to purchase what they needed and that was the end of that. On the other hand, our now *gentle-as-a-puppy-dog* captain more than likely received orders from his superiors to purchase everything he could find. The reason for this is that they could transport any amount of merchandise to any area of the country that they wanted. After all, it was the government, and who was going to question them?

Although it sounded good theoretically, circumstances could always change at the drop of a hat. That was why the government would rather receive its share in the mountains (their "protection" percentage). In the mountains, anything that transpired there stayed there, be it murder, mayhem, burning down entire villages, or all transactions. Outside the mountains, they could potentially expose any chink that they might have in their armor, so to speak.

What must be understood is that there are different factions at every level of government, and some are downright enemies of each other. Each one is *always* looking for a bigger piece of the pie, and it is as simple as that. If an enemy faction can be flushed down the proverbial toilet (as it were) and be replaced by the flusher, that's just business.

CHAPTER 28

Heavy Cash, *El Voludo*, Bushwhackers

Juanito had weighed all the merchandise taken to the cave on an old balance scale he had been using for years. It could only weigh up to fifty kilos at a time, but that was good enough. They had harvested a little over one thousand kilos of marijuana. At US$ 50 per kilo, the math was not hard to do, it came out to a little over fifty thousand dollars, a drop in the bucket when taking into consideration the overall haul from just that region. Nevertheless, for the average farmer, that was an unfathomable fortune that was simply beyond belief. It also meant that the new captain was carrying some unbelievably heavy cash on his person!

Those hillbillies who robbed their neighbors of their harvest and money had to be aware of this—if they were still around, that is. During all the chaos that ensued when the new captain first arrived, it was hard to say if any of the robbing, bushwhacking hillbillies had stuck around. In any case, none of the hillbillies who had elected to receive hard cash were dropping their guard. They requested military escorts wherever they went until they had finalized their business with the government.

Omar was not any different. Now that he was back at the cave and had counted out the cash in front of the guys, it was incumbent upon him to divide by twenty. After all, twenty was the original number of guys on the crew. Omar and the four guys did not have the slightest clue about their perilous situation. Notwithstanding, he realized that anything was possible because he knew how cruel Juanito could be.

Around 11:30 a.m. the next day, Omar sent two of the guys out to meet the helicopter. They were to remain at the forest's edge until it was well within sight. That's when they would come out running, leaving their weapons behind so as not to instill fear in the helicopter crew. Upon reaching the clearing, they would wave at the *voludo* and then simply wait for it to land.

The chopper espied the guys, circled a couple of times, then landed. Omar's two envoys then related to the pilot and the crew that they were to set the copter at the foot of the slope. Once there, they would help Omar and the others bring the merchandise down from the cave and start loading up

Our two guys were ordered to hop on board and, in a flash, were at the slope's foot. Just as the cumbersome loading task was about to begin, suddenly, and seemingly out of nowhere, rapid gunfire started raining down upon them. It had to be one of those thieving, bushwhacking hillbilly gangs! The bullets were coming from two directions, from above and from below. They were caught in the crossfire!

Omar and his two guys were still at the cave's entrance and *momentarily* safe. Those below were getting the worst of it. The pilot immediately radioed for backup and then caught a bullet in the head. He keeled over, having sacrificed his life for the enrichment of others. The other two soldiers bravely answered the flying lead but were seriously outmanned. Omar's two envoys were at the soldiers' side and had their weapons with them but were frightened beyond belief. They had never been in a firefight before and only half-heartedly fought back. Omar, from above, managed to get off several shots.

In less than five minutes, though, two more choppers appeared over the forest canopy and began hailing down bullets on the murderous attackers. Everything ended as quickly as it had begun. The attackers simply melted into the forest. One of the two choppers hovered over the one that had earlier set down at the foot of the slope while the other kept circling the area from above. They did not trust those bushwhacking hillbillies!

*****

Dear Reader,

This story took place circa 1985. If it had taken place thirty years later, those helicopters probably would have been shot down with bazookas! Case in point: In December 2015, a Mexican marine helicopter was shot down over the hills behind Culiacán, Sinaloa. Those hills were controlled by El Chapo's people, and it was shot down by a bazooka!

Furthermore, most Mexican military equipment comes from the USA. Although it's not state of the art (it's from that which was used ten to fifteen years earlier), it is still very deadly. In other words, the chopper downed by El Chapo's people was not a fossilized contraption from half a century ago. Moreover, most Mexican military pilots are trained in the USA.

CHAPTER 29

Roping Down, Attackers, Lots of Tortillas

After several seconds, four soldiers fast-roped down from the hovering chopper. As soon as they hit the ground, their chopper sped off with a few more soldiers still on board to aid the other chopper. They were determined to seek out and kill the attackers or to at least keep them at bay while the other chopper was loaded with the coveted merchandise. After a good long while, the chopper with the dead pilot was loaded, so one of the other choppers set down beside it. The pilot from that one, along with one soldier, climbed into the loaded whirlybird and flew off to unload and then return. The pilot's death would absolutely incur wrath among his fellow soldiers.

Meanwhile, the soldiers who remained, along with Omar and his four colleagues, would load the helicopter that was left behind. The third one would continue to circle widely overhead affording the men below sorely needed protection while the other sped off to unload and break the bad news.

Surprisingly, the soldiers who remained behind to help load the rest of the merchandise onto the helicopter remained quiet and stoic. Omar could only speculate that the captain would be given a full account of everything that transpired once they were back on San Vicente's esplanade.

As the chopper eased down at said esplanade with Omar and the other four on board, everything looked peaceful. The captain and some privates were even barbecuing a big chunk of beef! On a

86

table, they had placed all the trimmings and a *lot* of tortillas, both corn and flour.

The soldiers that had been on the helicopter immediately approached the captain, waiting for instructions. He simply ordered them to be at ease and to eat heartily once the food was ready. They happily obliged but knew they would be thoroughly questioned later about what happened at the cave. They were acutely cognizant that the captain had to have been briefed by the helicopter crew who had been ferrying the "goods."

At the cave again

Before lowering and then loading the last of the medicinal hemp into the *voludo* (chopper), Omar had apprised the soldiers below that he and his four colleagues needed to remove their scant personal belongings from the cave. Once in the cave, he let them have it.

"So you suckers want an equal share of the *goma*, right? Well, let me tell you something: *you'll be lucky to leave these hills alive!* After that blatant act of underwear-shitting cowardice you displayed just a few minutes ago, what makes you think the captain is going to keep protecting you? He might even confiscate your share of the money!"

By the look on his face and the tone of his voice, the four almost-trembling *wanna-be millionaires* could barely muster up the wherewithal to ask, "So now what?"

"So now what?" mockingly retorted Omar. "Your immediate fate is in my hands, and I could advise the captain to have you four good-for-nothings summarily executed." All four guys fell on their knees and beseeched Omar to give them one more chance.

"One more chance?" he replied. "Listen to me- and listen well. You are plumb out of chances! What we need to do is come to an agreement regarding your immediate future." They were all sobbing and fearful. Before Omar could even proceed though, they told him to just keep the money and the *goma* and to just get them home alive! He happily accepted their proposal.

"I'll talk to the captain," he replied. "Now let's get the freak out of here!"

CHAPTER 30

Back to the Esplanade a Few Minutes into the Future

"*A dead pilot! You mean they killed one of our pilots?*" unbelievably lamented the dead pilot's companions. "Those hillbilly bastards murdered our *compadre*! They murdered him!" they kept grievously crying out. Crying out and just as emotionally distraught as his men was the captain. Suddenly, as if hit by a bolt of lightning, the captain came to his senses. He realized that those renegade mountain men represented a minority of the local yokels, and that was the extent of it.

Cognizant that he could not let his emotions get the best of him, he got back on the right keel. His superiors expected him to piece together that which he had destroyed, and he was determined to be successful. He ordered the men to calm down. "Everything will come full circle in due time," he said. "I want these savages to pay for what they did just as badly as you, but we must do it military style. Discipline, men. Discipline over and above everything else will enable us to avenge his murder." To be sure, the captain's superiors did not share his spirit of vengeance. They could have cared less. The only thing they were concerned about was lining their pockets. Lower-ranking soldiers were expendable.

After placing the pilot in a body bag and gathering the men around him to say a short prayer, he had the poor fellow flown to

Choix, Sinaloa, for a proper burial. Choix was also where the nearest fort was located. The captain and almost all the troops stood in formation, saluting, as the helicopter lifted up and then sped off. Four troops had been left at the ready, posted in strategic positions in case some renegades tried to snipe them.

The hillbillies who were at the esplanade doffed their hats and bowed their heads in a token of respect at the informal *wake* if you will. Whether all of them felt it in their hearts was another thing altogether. Word was bound to get around about how these local yokels seemingly manifested deference and sadness for the enemy.

CHAPTER 31

The Night Before or from Another Angle

The night before at the cave as Omar was showing the guys the money, he asked them several questions and painted a scenario. The scenario he painted was not hard to understand, and the questions he posed were quite elementary. He made it quite clear that Juanito would not tolerate being made a fool of, in the first place, and, in the second place, he would put the full blame on his (Omar's) shoulders. Long story short, Juanito would not rest until Omar had suffered a horrible death.

"Do I make myself quite clear, guys?" asked Omar. "My life will *never* be the same! Notwithstanding, it's either this or getting swindled by Juanito, and I'm quite sure none of us want to get swindled. Does everyone agree?" Everyone nodded their head in agreement. Then practically in unison, they asked Omar about the sizable amount of *goma* (opium) that had been harvested. "It's all in my backpack," he answered. "Now let me ask all of you a question. Once the big boss man realizes he has been taken, don't you understand that my life won't be worth a plug nickel? He is going to want my scalp, and it is as simple as that!"

His words reflected the troubled countenance on his face. "I don't believe any of you guys, not one, comprehends the seriousness of my situation. Every single one of you will be able to return to your homes but not me!"

"How do you know he won't come looking for us?" they chimed in.

"Because all of you are greenhorns!" Omar testily replied. "Even if he does, you won't be able to tell him anything other than that you got paid for your several months of backbreaking work. If, and when, he asks you where I am, just tell him the truth—*parts unknown* because no one will know my whereabouts and that's exactly how I want it." The guys once again asked about the *goma.*

"Basically, you guys want to know how it's gonna be divided, right?" queried Omar.

"We already know!" they responded. "Every man is gonna get his fair share!"

Omar folded his hands behind his back, smiled, looked down at his hardened, callous-encrusted feet still laced into their tire-tread sandals, then began slowly walking around the cave while seemingly contemplating the ceiling. He was formulating a response that would leave them frightened and desperate.

"Well, it's pretty obvious that you guys already have your minds made up. If that's the case, then we'll just divvy up all the *goma,* then afterward you are on your own. If you don't have any qualms about leaving me in the lurch, then I'll just reciprocate!"

"What do you mean?" they asked, with a look of shared confusion on their faces.

"I mean that I refuse to stick out my neck for you ungrateful suckers any longer! You can take all your money, and that of your sixteen buddies, along with your share of the *goma,* and get back down to the coast on your own! Do I make myself crystal clear?"

"Just a goddamn minute, dude!" one of them shot back. "That's not the deal we struck with Juanito. He told us, *no,* he promised us, that he'd get us back home after harvest. Now since he is no longer here, that responsibility is on your shoulders!"

"Oh, really?" replied Omar sarcastically. "Let's see here. Let me contemplate this situation for about half a second. Naah, I abdicate!"

The four guys were quietly taken aback. The silence of the cave was deafening. "So now what?" they asked. Omar didn't utter a word. Instead, he strode straight over to Juanito's old balance scale to begin weighing out the *goma* into twenty-one parcels knowing full well that the guys were eventually going to stop him. Nonetheless, he was going to play it out as much as possible just to prove he wasn't bluffing.

"So that's how it's gonna be?" they chided.

Omar remained silent, carefully weighing out each parcel and fully expecting them, at any moment, to relent. They did not. Finally, after he was finished, and with silence still reigning supreme inside their labyrinth, he reminded them that a helicopter would be arriving close by to pick up the *other* merchandise the next morning. Two of them would go out to meet it and give them some instructions. Those instructions would be given to them right before they left.

Omar was expecting them to whine and complain about two of them being sent out to meet the other chopper, but they didn't say a word. He was stymied but kept as cool as a cucumber. Morning was soon upon them and, after a good long while, he chose the two who were going to meet the chopper. He gave them their instructions and then sent them on their way. He patiently waited for them to climb down to the foot of the slope, then watched as they disappeared into the forest, rifles in tow. Now it was simply a matter of waiting for the helicopter to show up. Meanwhile, Omar and his two colleagues would continue silently enjoying the safety of their lair.

In due course, the distinct, mechanical sound of whirlybird blades was heard, getting louder every second. Omar ran over to the boulders at the cave's entrance and peered through them from an angle that would give him a full view of the helicopter when it landed. His two "colleagues" were right there, next to him, peering out as well.

All three observed the two envoys run out from within the forest to greet the helicopter as it landed in the clearing. Their eagle eyes were still upon them as they conferred with the pilot and then got on board. As it sped toward the slope, Omar and his two *sidekicks* got ready to lower the first pack of "medicinal herb." After securing it on one end of a sturdy rope, they waited for the copter to land, and land it did. As they were about to start lowering the first part of the stash, *all hell broke loose!*

Automatic gunfire from seemingly everywhere exploded! Omar's two buddies dashed into the safety of the cave leaving Omar by himself behind the boulders. "What a couple of real chickens!" he said to himself. "These two suckers both have a yellow streak running down their back, and I'm quite sure their two feathered buddies do as well!" he muttered under his breath.

CHAPTER 32

Brain Matter, Cowards, Gunfire

From his vantage point, he was able to observe everything that was happening below. He took in the very moment when the young pilot was shot in the left temple. What he could not see, however, because of his angle, was how the powerful high-caliber bullet had torn clean through his head and out the other temple. Upon exiting, it took a major chunk of skull and brain matter, horribly depositing it inside the chopper. Some of it even stained the back of one of the soldiers as he was getting out to engage the bushwhackers! It was a gut-wrenching sight.

Omar then ran inside the cave, grabbed his weapon, fleetingly observed the two cowards as they were putting the palms of their hands over their ears to lessen the thunderous noise of the gunfire, then dashed outside. He managed to scream, "Cowards!" at the two paralyzed, trembling *wanna-be-millionaires* who wouldn't have left the safety of the cave for all the tea in China.

Finding himself another opening in the boulders that afforded him a different angle down below, he spotted a couple of the opposing hill folk. They were at the forest's edge mostly firing toward the chopper. Now and then, they shot toward the cave and would hit nothing but boulders. One of the hillbillies looked familiar.

Who is this guy? thought Omar. *I've seen him before!*

He then opened fire on those same two hillbillies who melted back into the forest forest. He was quite certain he had shot at least one of those murderers, but there was no way to confirm it unless either a body or a lot of blood was later found.

As soon as the other two helicopters were spotted, the bushwhackers disappeared, and that was that. Now Omar's four cowardly companions would be duly chastised—verbally at least—by the soldiers. Surprisingly, the soldiers who had stayed behind to help load the "other" merchandise onto the helicopter remained quiet and stoic. Omar could only speculate that the captain would be given a full account of all that happened once they were back on San Vicente's esplanade.

As the chopper eased down at said esplanade with Omar and the other four on board, everything looked peaceful. The captain and some privates were even barbecuing a big chunk of beef! On a table, they had placed all the trimmings.

The soldiers that had been on the helicopter immediately approached the captain, waiting for instructions. He just ordered them to be at ease and to eat heartily once the food was ready. They happily obliged but knew they would be thoroughly questioned later about what transpired at the cave. They were acutely cognizant that the captain had to have been briefed by the helicopter crew who had been ferrying the "goods."

CHAPTER 33

Juanito and Temo

At the crack of dawn, Juanito and Temo carried the guys up to the higher ground, well away from the beaten path, and erased all traces of their presence. Juanito stoked a smokeless fire to heat up some of the food Doña (Donia) Lola had prepared. These guys needed to have at least three meals a day for several days running before they could even entertain the thought of attempting to get back down to the coast.

The delicious aroma of breakfast warming up had them salivating (much like Pavlov's famous pooches). The anticipation of machaca with eggs and potatoes, refried beans with melted cheese, and finally flour tortillas titillating their taste buds was about all they could handle. They couldn't even remember the last time they had eaten flour tortillas! (Sidenote: In Northwestern Mexico, flour tortillas are considered to be a real treat since corn tortillas are usually served with every meal.) Juanito and Temo even served them and kept warming up more tortillas as needed. Everyone was served piping hot coffee with plenty of sugar when they finished.

After devouring their breakfast, the guys had their limbs, hands, and feet examined by Juanito and Temo (country doctors!). Of the sixteen guys, eight would be ready to make a go for the coast within five or six days. As for the other eight, it would take many days longer. They had suffered a wide range of noncritical injuries but were injured nonetheless. There was a lot of soreness and swelling. A couple of them had even suffered split soles. They would all eventually and completely recover—physically that is. Mentally and emotionally was a whole different matter, rest assured.

After six days had passed, Juanito felt the previously mentioned eight injured fellows were ready to walk the remaining twenty-some miles to the highway leading back to Los Mochis. He and Temo had packed them up plenty of food. (Temo had ridden back home on his steed a few days earlier to pick up fresh supplies.) Before they set out though, Juanito gave them his all-too-customary lecture.

"Alright, fellas, gather around closely because I need to give you a heads-up. This is the last leg of your journey back home, and I know you all want to get there." Their ears perked up as they stood around him in a semicircle in their ragged clothes, tattered cowboy hats, and tire-tread sandals. They all looked extremely thin and gaunt, and their hair was way overdue for a serious visit to the barbershop. Plus, they all needed a no-nonsense, razor-sharp shave. To boot, their nostril hairs had become entwined with their overgrown mustaches, and their ear hairs had become jungle-like in density.

"Every one of you needs to understand that Temo is going to be the only one giving orders up until the time you board the bus. Anyone who falls behind on the road will either need to catch up or get to the highway on his own accord. He is not going to wait for stragglers.

"If that happens to any one of you, just remember what I've already told you countless times. On the other side of the highway is a creek. Remember? Find a good hiding place in the creek where no one can see you, take off all your rags, throw them in the bushes, then completely bathe yourself, and wash your hair with the toiletries that each one of you brought along from the coast. Next, completely shave off your unsightly beards and mustaches, and finally, brush your teeth! If any of you brought along scissors and a mirror, make sure you trim all those unsightly nostril and ear hairs although you could probably do better by just shaving off those ear hairs!

"Afterward put on the clean clothes you brought along from the coast then your clean tennis shoes. Right now, before you leave, I am going to give each one of you your bus fare to get back home. This way, if *you do* get separated, you can still make it back—as long as you don't get snagged by the soldiers!

"Well, that's all I have to say. I'll see you guys in two or three weeks back on the coast with your well-earned money. Stay close to Temo and follow his orders. Off with you now!"

They walked off with Temo leading the way. Juanito observed them until they blended into the forest. "Sorry, guys," he said to himself, "but this will serve you all as a great life lesson—you *and* your partners. This time, I am keeping everything, even Omar's share." He chuckled to himself as he turned and walked back toward the other eight guys who were still healing.

Temo and the other eight had eaten a hearty breakfast but hadn't finished it all, so he warmed up some corn tortillas on the still-hot embers. Oddly enough, Juanito, unlike most people, wasn't crazy about flour tortillas. There was plenty to be had, but he was a strict corn man. As he warmed up the corn tortillas, the snoring of the eight remaining warriors made him smile. *Poor suckers!* he thought.

CHAPTER 34

Temo and the Fearsome Eight/8

Having bid farewell, "the Fearsome 8" strode away at a crisp pace with Temo at the lead on horseback. He was no fool! He knew that crisp pace wouldn't last long. They were walking along the upper embankment of an arroyo (creek) that would eventually feed into the Río Quintana about a mile before they hit the highway. It was the Río's last tributary and a good eighteen-mile trek. Temo knew the country like the back of his hand.

There were small boulders and rocks scattered throughout the breadth and length of said creek, so they were quite fortunate to be able to stride along its upper embankment which was *comparatively* rock and boulder free. Their ceaseless striding (behind Temo's horse to be sure) was always slightly downhill. Since Temo's *mighty steed* was freely fertilizing all the ground behind him and occasionally cutting explosive farts, our mighty warriors had to walk very carefully. Otherwise, they'd have equine road apple smeared all over their tire-tread sandals, between their toes, and sandwiched between the soles of their feet and the rubber below them. Even worse, a few of our merry men who were following Temo's steed much too close got sprayed in the face with flatulence bombs and learned right away to keep their distance.

Needless to say, a few of them were forced to navigate their way down to the water to rinse off their feet (and faces) in the ice-cold pure water while they were able to do so. Some more than once!

Walking, with all the horse poop between their toes, etc., felt uncomfortable, gross, and unclean. When finished with the rinsing, they scrambled back up the embankment and trotted until they caught up with Temo and the guys. After their turd-laden experience, they didn't at all mind bringing up the very end of the rear. The further from the horse's butt, the better.

After trekking ten miles, Temo ordered everyone to stop and rest under a giant sabino tree, make a fire, and warm up some of the vittles they had brought along. He took the horse down to the creek to drink water and afterward tied him to a fallen sycamore tree at the edge of the creek where there was plenty of fresh green grass and fresh tender shoots coming out of the well-watered soil. Then he noticed some fresh, ominous tracks—jaguar tracks. They belonged to an adult female and her two cubs.

He followed the tracks for about fifty yards down the creek until they lurched up the embankment and disappeared into the thick bush. He wasn't overly worried though because he was carrying an AK-47 and a 9-mm pistol. Nonetheless, it was his duty to go back and warn the guys to keep their heads up and stay on their toes in case there were any more jags around. If there were, they wouldn't be close by at any rate, but it was always better to be safe than sorry.

These felines, as well as pumas and onzas, liked to stealthily post high up in sabino trees and wait for something succulent to amble on by. Although it was rare for them to attack humans, it wasn't unheard of. When it did occasionally happen (usually once or twice every few decades), it was always an older cat whose prowess, agility, and speed had diminished to the point that it had no choice other than to attack slow-moving humans who, nevertheless, offered an easy meal.

Notwithstanding, whenever this happened, all the mountain folk would get together (even old enemies) and set traps, divide themselves into hunting parties, and with hunting dogs look for the killer cat who would eventually be shot and killed or trapped. If the killer feline was never found, that only meant that he or she had fled the area because they were frightened. Big cats are absolutely scared of humans and would much rather stay away from us.

Returning to his horse which he had left in equine heaven, joyfully grazing, and dropping horse chips without a care in the world after having drank pure, cold creek water for several minutes with seemingly no end in sight, he decided to let him indulge a while longer while he hiked up the embankment so he could tell the guys about the jag tracks.

After having apprised them while taking in their predictable reaction which began with all of them spreading out and gazing upward almost expecting to see a jag or some other feline up in the sabino tree ready to pounce, Temo stated quite succinctly that all dangerous felines were long gone.

"They heard us coming from hundreds of meters away, gents, so don't worry about it too much. I had originally planned for us to stick around here for a few hours and then pull out so we could get to where the creek empties into the river right at sunset, but I hadn't counted on the jag tracks. That changed the whole equation. Instead, we'll pull out *right now*, and when we get to the river, we'll hike up a small hill which will enable us to see everything happening below us. We don't want to be surprised, much less ambushed. Do I make myself clear?" Everyone nodded their heads in serious agreement.

"Alright then. Let me get a bite to eat because I am starving, and that food you guys warmed up really smells good! Meanwhile, wash those dishes and repack the food you didn't warm up while I wipe this frying pan clean with this flour tortilla. While I'm stuffing my face, you can begin getting everything ready for our several-mile trek. When I'm through licking my chops, I'll go and retrieve my steed."

CHAPTER 35

Happily Snorting, Mormons, Green Parrots

Fifteen minutes later, Temo was on the creek bed untying his horse from the fallen tree. With the rein in his hand, he was about to lead the old boy back to where the guys were, but the horse had a different idea. Forget about the adage of taking a horse to water and not being able to make it drink. On the contrary, in this case, it was the beast taking the human to water (which was just a few steps away) and, for a couple of minutes at least, turning into a flesh-and-blood water pump.

Once our trustworthy steed had drank to its heart's content, Temo continued leading it back to where the guys were. Dropping road apples all the way back and happily snorting with its muzzle pointed at an upward angle, while playfully swishing its reddish-black tail back and forth, this cheerful, fortunate equine felt like *the leader of the pack*. Not more than ten minutes later, our well-fed guys were ambling down the trail with Temo at the lead mounted on his trusty beast.

They took two fifteen-minute breaks along the way and observed quite a few roadrunners, quail, and ground squirrels whipping on by, some coming from the creek bed, others going toward it. Pine trees were becoming scarcer and scarcer, but the mighty oak, as well as other giants, were still on guard duty. In fact, even a few cottonwood trees were manifesting their awesome presence right along the creek bed together with chaparral-like vegetation, which was slowly starting to spread out, or reclaim, if you will, the turf it had lost to higher, more well-watered elevation.

About two kilometers before the creek emptied into the Río Quintana, they espied several Tarahumaras crisply walking toward them. They were Mormons! Dressed in well-ironed slacks with the usual white shirt and tie, these five young men carried briefcases filled with the Church of Latter-day Saints literature (in Spanish, of course) and were there proselytizing. They wanted to engage the guys in conversation, but Temo politely declined. Nonetheless, they managed to pass out several pamphlets before continuing their journey, happily smiling. As they were about to pull away in their tire-tread sandals, they related to the guys how they were from this area and were on their way to their village where other Tarahumara Mormon converts awaited them and where they (i.e., Temo and his crew) were always welcome.

Finally, right before they turned away to continue striding, they told the guys that they had encountered several highway roadblocks on their way up from Los Mochis. They had exited the rural bus just a few kilometers away, right on the bridge where our merry men would be crossing after dark. These Tarahumara had read our guys like a book and were truly concerned for them.

Once the Tarahumaras had turned and were striding away, a huge cloud of at least a few hundred small, green parrots with red markings seemingly appeared out of nowhere. Whistling and squawking with unabated energy, coupled with the furious, incessant flapping of their wings, they spread over the dirt road just a few feet above the surface and disappeared into the creek below. That might have been their nesting area because the squawking, whistling, and trills continued unabated from the canopy of the many oaks rising from the creek.

When they were about a kilometer away from the bridge, with at least three hours of sunlight left, Temo took them up a low hill covered with plenty of brush and oak trees. They would remain there until it was completely dark. Temo tied his steed in the middle of a grove of black oak and told the guys to relax and just kick it. In a flash, all the guys were in a prone position, some smoking and everyone quietly chatting. Temo said they could smoke after they related to him what Juanito had told them about smoking in the woods.

He told them that since this a was well-transited area, not far from the highway, people, whether on foot or on beast, would smoke, so as to not worry about it. He once again explained to them what they were going to do after crossing the highway and finding a well-hidden place next to flowing water. There they would bathe, shave, brush their teeth, cut their hair, and put on fresh clothes, tennis shoes, and baseball caps.

CHAPTER 36

Clean Clothes, Worn-Out Clothes, and Merchandise

Once darkness had completely set in, it was time to move out. About an hour before, Temo had ordered the guys to ready their gear, keeping it within arm's reach, and to have a final smoke because when it got dark a lit cigarette, much less a match, could be spotted from a great distance. If they were bathed and dressed in clean clothes, it would be a different story, but they obviously weren't. He explained to them that occasionally, either the police or the military would park a short distance, a hundred meters or so from the bridge they were going to cross from below and hide in the brush underneath it. They would then waylay anyone attempting to make their way through to the other side.

If they were caught wearing their old, worn-out clothes, it would be disastrous—a late-night bath accompanied by punches, kicks, and rifle butts to the rib cage would be next on the agenda. The reason for such a beating would be to attempt to extract information from them that would lead to arresting someone they knew who possessed merchandise. It goes without saying that if the unfortunate late-night travelers were busted carrying merchandise, it would be a whole new ballgame.

Being stopped and held with no merchandise on them meant that they would probably be released after a thorough whipping if they kept their mouths shut. On the other hand, if merchandise was discovered on them, and they refused to talk, they could very well be executed right then and there. Notwithstanding, in this case, that was not in the cards.

About a hundred meters before getting to the bridge, Temo had the boys hunker down in the creek, amid the giant oaks, leaving his weapon with them. He ordered them to remain completely quiet then proceeded forward crossing the width of the bridge from above. Continuing on the trail for at least another hundred meters, he gently pulled on the reins to stop the horse, dismounted, and just stood there for several minutes in the darkness with the reins in his hand. His ears were perked taking in all sounds.

After a while, he began to make his way back, a few meters at a time, walking the horse and then stopping to see if he could hear any voices resonating from beneath the bridge. If he did, then he wouldn't make his way back to the guys until whoever was under the bridge had taken off. If it was the cops or the military, he would know from the get-go because they always made a lot of noise when moving out.

When he had slowly but surely gotten to within twenty or so meters from the bridge, he stopped and just listened, remaining as still as a statue. His well-trained, trusty steed reciprocated. After a good, long while when he was thoroughly convinced that everything was safe, and there was no law enforcement present, he mounted his horse and continued at a trot until he got to where the boys were hunkered down.

Silently dismounting, he approached them so quietly on foot that they didn't even notice he was there until he was upon them. Startled for a fleeting moment, Temo quickly and quietly told them to hush and stay still with a loud whisper.

"Okay, listen up!" he said, still whispering. "I am going to *silently* hike back up the embankment and *silently* walk my horse back down. The key word here is *silently.* If you understand me just keep quiet. Anyone who doesn't understand, just whisper, 'No,' loudly enough for it to reach my ears, and we'll talk about it." Everyone remained silent. In two shakes of a lamb's tail, Temo was back with his trusty steed.

"Now listen to me well!" he whispered. "I am going to walk my horse down to the bridge, and you are going to follow me remaining twenty paces behind, walking single file. This way no one will get lost. When we are all under the bridge, we will keep on walking forward in the same fashion that got us there. Understood? Alright, let's go!" he whispered.

CHAPTER 37

Treading Lightly, Skunks, a Transformation

With his horse's rein in his right hand, Temo began gingerly walking forward, carefully placing one foot ahead of the other and making sure to make as little noise as possible. With a sweeping gesture, he directed the guys to follow him. They knew at this point to tread lightly and to only whisper. Before they knew it, they were passing under the bridge barely making a sound.

They kept treading forward, always keeping at the top of their mind that making even a little noise could potentially be their undoing. About twenty-five yards past the bridge, Temo slowly raised his left arm and loudly whispered for them to stop and remain completely still.

"I smell a skunk!" he whispered. "No one move, or we could very well get doused with skunk spray!"

Everyone became as still as stone. At that precise moment, a new quarter moon emerged from behind some clouds, slightly illuminating the landscape. After a minute or so, Temo observed a good-sized skunk barely eight feet in front of him with its tail in the trigger position. He apprised them once more with a loud whisper not to move then told them about the skunk almost at his feet.

After what seemed like an eternity, the damn polecat lowered its tail and scampered into the brush. During that short interim, a couple of trucks passed over the bridge, but fortunately, no one observed them. As soon as that infernal varmint disappeared into the vegetation, Temo, with a circular motion of his left arm, gestured for everyone to continue forward.

After lightly treading for another 150 meters, Temo raised his hand and, in a low voice, told them to stop and gather around him. "For all means and purposes," said he, "we are now out of danger as far as the law goes. The cops or soldiers never wander into the forest this deep at night because they know they can get sniped. At any rate, we will now climb up the southern embankment and walk a couple of miles to a creek that is just a few hundred yards from the bus stop. Once we get to the creek, you are all going to undertake a transformation," he laughingly exclaimed.

"What do you mean a transformation?" apprehensively queried the guys.

"Don't get your tail feathers ruffled!" shot back Temo in a low voice, gritting his teeth. "You are all going to cut your hair, trim your beards, brush your teeth, bathe, shave, then put on the clean clothes and tennis shoes, you've been toting along with you for months. That's the transformation!" The guys regained their composure and remained completely silent.

After climbing the embankment, they softly walked south for about an hour and a half, with Temo in the lead on horseback until they had gotten to the creek that he had told them about. The guys were starting to get the hang of walking silently in the forest at night!

Once there, Temo dismounted and led his horse to the creek so it could drink water. He then asked the boys to gather around him so he could tell them exactly what they were going to do.

"I know it's dark, but with the moonlight, everyone should be able to make out that spot in the creek right below those big rocks from where the water is gushing out into the pool below. It's like a natural shower! That is where you are going to bathe, one at a time. Why one at a time, you might ask? It's because if things get dangerous, and you are all butt naked, that would be one hell of a situation!

"Although there is no law enforcement here at night, there could always be some local yokels armed to the teeth wandering around who wouldn't hesitate to rob us, if given half a chance, especially if you are in your birthday suits. But that ain't going to happen!

"I am going to tie my horse behind that cluster of boulders over yonder and climb up on top of it. This way, I can be scanning the landscape by the light of the silvery quarter moon while you gents bathe *one at a time*! Let's be clear about that. At any rate, if anything unexpected happens, I'll advise you from my perch, and we'll take it from there. More than likely, I'll tell you guys to beat it into the woods and to make yourself scarce while I deal with any potential usurper.

"In fact, now that I think of it, all of you except he who will be bathing and another one of you who will be handing him his toiletries and clothing will be hiding in the shadows in case anything does transpire. Better to be safe than sorry. Now that we've gotten that straightened out, who wants to bathe first? No volunteers? No biggy! I'll choose. I'm going to show you how it's done from beginning to end so scoot close and watch me as best you can."

CHAPTER 38

Young Whippersnapper, Pool's Edge, Rural Bus Stop

He randomly chose a guy who looked so tired, he was about to keel over. Directing him to the edge of the pool, he ordered him to sit on his haunches. Taking out some big scissors from his jacket pocket, he proceeded to cut the young whippersnapper's hair, then trim his beard. Next, he ordered him to take off all his dirty, worn-out garbs and sandals, roll them into a tight bundle, then hurl them as far as he could from the creek.

Grabbing the guy's makeshift backpack, he took out his clean clothes, some tennis shoes, and a big towel, set them aside, then removed all the toiletries, including a razorblade and comb, put everything into a big plastic bag, then ordered the now butt naked, shivering whippersnapper into the pool. The young man was at first reluctant, but when Temo threatened to push him in, he knew he had no choice and relented. Temo then ordered him to immerse himself completely in the freezing water and then to stand back up and walk over to the pool's edge.

When he was about two feet from Temo, he was told to stop. Temo then handed him some shampoo. When he was finished with that, he gave him some soap and a washcloth, followed by a toothbrush and toothpaste then finally the razorblade. After shaving, he was told to rinse himself off either by once again immersing himself or standing under the "natural" shower gushing out of the rocks. He chose the shower!

Next, Temo ordered him to come out of the pool, dry himself off, and get dressed. "That's how it's done troops!" declared Temo. "Now the ball is in your court. Just remember that only two at a time by the creek! The rest of you hide in the shadows. Meanwhile, I'll be on top of those boulders keeping watch. Shift it into high gear. Oh, I forgot to tell you. When you're bathed and dressed, go ahead, and take a nap behind the boulders I'll be perched on. Dawn is still a few hours away."

It took less than an hour for everyone to bathe, shave, etc. Soon everyone was sacked out behind the clump of boulders, snoring away as if they were home in bed. They were all extremely exhausted, fatigued, and spent. No one even smoked before putting themselves into a prone position and that was highly unusual because several of the guys really enjoyed their tobacco. That just goes to show you how burned out and jaded they were. Temo remained atop the boulder assemblage attempting to perceive and discern anything, within the strict limitations of the moonlight, which might be moving around in the surrounding landscape.

After Temo had woken them up well before the first light of dawn, he advised them to quickly make a fire, so they could warm up some tortillas and beef jerky. The first rays of dawn were accompanied by the chirping of birds and the mooing of a cow. Temo digested the whole majestic scenario as he had done innumerable times during his relatively short time on earth.

They only had four hundred meters to go before arriving at the bus stop. With food in their bellies and having gotten a few hours of sleep, they were walking spritely and smiling. How they wanted to get home to be their loved ones! Having bathed the night before and wearing clean duds made them feel brand-new. They were about to leave the worse several months of their life behind them, and it was a lesson sorely learned! Their pockets were empty, but so what? It was back to the only life they had ever known where they could feel secure and protected.

Temo ordered them to halt close to the periphery of the rural bus stop while they were still well within the forest and couldn't be seen by passing vehicles. "Okay, listen up!" he barked, as he dismounted his horse with the reins in his left hand. "You are not all going to go on the same bus because it might look a little suspicious! Just think about it. Eight young guys boarding the bus at the same time, wearing crispy-clean clothes, everyone well-shaved, well-bathed, and every single one of you wearing clean tennis shoes to boot! That could raise some eyebrows, and we wouldn't want that now, would we?

"If some eyebrows were raised, and we were to hit a roadblock, those same raised eyebrows, if they like sticking their nose into other people's business, could tell the law that you look mighty suspicious." Everyone nodded their heads in agreement.

"So you are going to have to board the bus four at a time which means two buses will have to be boarded. A bus usually drives by every thirty to forty minutes so all of you will be out of here in no time flat." Temo chose the two foursomes and quickly told one of them to stand near the paved road's edge. The sun had just majestically risen over the horizon, so it was a new day.

Within an hour and a half, all our troopers were long gone, and Temo was on his steed going back along the same route that had gotten him there. None the worse for the wear, our eight young whippersnappers were elated to be going back to civilization and three hot meals a day. Not one *ever* wanted to go back to the Sierra.

CHAPTER 39

Bubbling Water, Dense Vegetation, Slow Motion

On the way back, slumber started besetting Temo. It was late morning, and he was absolutely in need of some serious rest seeing as how he had been up all night long perched atop that pile of boulders keeping guard. Espying up ahead a pleasant-looking area located on a bend in the stream, immersed in giant oak and cottonwood trees with the crystal waters of the stream swiftly flowing through the almost-dead center, he opted for that spot.

As the bubbling water incessantly flowed ever westward toward its destination, it would dart in and out of the shadows created by the forest canopy which was always gently swaying thanks to the usually mild breeze. At certain times of the year, this same breeze would blow with hurricane-like force. When they were out of the shadows, seemingly playful rays of sunlight tenderly caressed the leaves and branches of the different trees while making their way downward toward the stream where they intermittently shined on the water's surface making it sparkle.

Temo carefully ambled down the creek's embankment without dismounting and rode in several yards till he was completely camouflaged by the dense vegetation. He chose a small, slightly elevated clearing a few feet from the ever-flowing water. It was covered with lush, intensely green dichondra. The sun's rays filtered in unimpeded through a wide circular opening in the canopy.

Dismounting next to the clearing, he walked his horse away several feet, then at the stream's edge, firmly tied him to an Aliso sapling. The thirsty equine immediately began to siphon in water through its pursed lips. He steadily drew in water without missing a beat. He drank and drank to its heart's content then began to graze on all the green that caught its fancy.

Temo slowly laid himself on the lush, green grass using his rolled-up jacket as a pillow. When he was in an almost prone position, face up, he stretched out his arms and legs feeling the stretch even in his shoulders and hips. Suddenly, it was as if he was moving in slow motion. He deeply exhaled then slowly sank down into the carpet of dichondra overlaid, as it was, on creek sand which slightly gave way to the weight of his body.

Gradually raising his eyes upward and setting his sights on the opening, he beheld shafts of sunlight brilliantly cascading downward, ever downward, till they either caressed the flowing water or the sand with its patches of green. A few even gently stroked his forehead and chest as he descended into a deep, well-deserved slumber. Midafternoon, he was awoken from his sleep by a raucous cacophony of *caaw-caaw-caawing* from several crows who were pursuing a hawk who had apparently flown too close to their nesting area.

He instinctually sat up, his mind still not even in first gear, trying to assess the situation. As he gradually detached himself from the deep cloud of drowsiness in which he had been pleasantly enveloped, he was able to mentally and then physically situate himself. Contemplating the situation, as he became more and more awake and cognizant, he realized he was quite famished!

He stood up, stretched, and yawned, then slowly walked over to his horse while still yawning. He opened the saddlebag and pulled out some beef jerky and refried beans in a pouch along with a few corn tortillas. In no time flat he had a small, smokeless fire going. With adroit hands, he put the beans and jerky in a small frying pan and then placed it on the embers. As soon as it started to sizzle, he removed it from the fire and then began warming up the tortillas directly on some red-hot embers, constantly flipping them so they wouldn't get hard much less burn.

In ten minutes, he was licking his chops and wiping his mouth with his left shirt sleeve. Sitting next to the fire, he rolled up a home-grown tobacco cigarette, lit it, then contently puffed away. Right before he stood up, he loudly burped a couple of times and then tossed the half-smoked cigarette into the stream. Next, he took the frying pan and a couple of utensils to the stream, scrubbed them with sand, rinsed them, then laid them on a branch to dry.

After a couple of minutes, he doused the fire, placed the frying pan and utensils into the saddlebags, untied the horse, mounted it, and in a few seconds was up on the trail, ambling along, getting closer to home. There were still a few hours of sunlight left, but he was in no rush since he didn't plan on seeing Juanito until the next day. He comfortably got home well after dark.

CHAPTER 40

Crack of Dawn, Chirping Birds, Machaca

Walking in the back door straight into the kitchen, his sense of smell was set head over heel by a scrumptious meal his mother had prepared him. She was sitting at the kitchen table smiling. "I just knew you'd be coming in tonight," she said.

"How do you do it, Mom? It's like you have a crystal ball at your disposal!" he chimed in. A half hour later, he had devoured his meal and was now on the back porch smoking one of his father's store-bought cigarettes and drinking a cup of coffee. His old man was soon sitting next to him. They contemplated the stars for a few minutes then began chatting. His father related to him how he had gone to see Juanito and his *patients* the day before and had also taken them three or four days of vittles. Looking his son square in the eye, he solemnly declared that Juanito needed to speak to him urgently and that he should leave at that crack of dawn. Wasting no time, Temo was laid out on his cot in less than ten minutes.

Well before the crack of dawn, Temo had already saddled his horse and was sitting at the kitchen table with his mother, sipping on a cup of piping hot coffee and munching on some sweet bread. In a few minutes, he was on his horse making his way toward Juanito and the injured parties. He reached their encampment when it was still quite early, and the birds were still chirping.

Upon arriving, Juanito laughingly greeted him and then asked him how everything had gone. Temo just gave him a smiling thumbs up and then mentioned what his father had told him.

"Before talking, let's have some breakfast," suggested Juanito. In ten minutes, he had warmed up some eggs, machaca, potatoes, beans, and flour tortillas on the fire that had been going nonstop since Temo had left with the eight other guys. The food had been made, of course, by Temo's mother (Doña [Donia] Lola). They *all* quietly ate, thoroughly enjoying the food. After finishing, everyone drank coffee, and a few guys smoked, including Temo.

"Time is passing, and a few of these guys are gonna need at least another week of rest and recovery before even trying to make it to the coast. We've got a good, hidden spot here, well above this hardly ever-used trail which means no one will ever spot us *or hear us* as long as we talk very quietly.

"I need for you to stay with these guys, Temo, until they are ready to roll. I'll make it worth your while, my friend, believe me. All eight automatic weapons will be yours plus five thousand pesos to boot. Of course, you'll have to take them to the highway like you did the other eight, but that's par for the course. Just do it at your speed. No rush, just make sure they all board the bus."

Temo concurred but was concerned for his parents because he did all the heavy work around the house and didn't want to leave them in the lurch by staying up here for several days in a row because, as it was, he had already been gone for more than a day. Juanito completely understood and advised him to ride back now and carry out whatever chores needed to be done and to be back within two days with plenty of food. Every couple of days he could always ride to check up on his parents just so long as he was back by nightfall.

CHAPTER 41

Tehueco, the Jesuits, and El Río Fuerte

Temo took off with his mind clicking trying to figure out how much money he and his parents could get for the guns because they desperately needed cash. The five thousand pesos would be put to good use as soon as those eight guys were out of his hair. Back in forty-eight hours with a load of prepared food, his idea was to ride back for more and quickly return when it started getting low. Every time he went, he would take one of the weapons.

As soon as he showed up after the forty-eight-hour hiatus, Juanito took off wishing him well. He had packed a healthy lunch and was now clipping along at top speed. He looked like an Olympic marathon walker and didn't plan to rest until he had gotten to the village of Tehueco nestled alongside the Fuerte River in Sinaloa.

Juanito cut straight across the forest in a west-by-southwest direction avoiding all trails. He knew the lay of the land like the back of his hand and would come out about one kilometer above Tehueco which was a mission village originally founded by the Jesuits centuries ago. He planned to sleep in the woods right next to the river, possibly even up in a cottonwood tree to play it safe and, in that manner, avoid any encounters with two-legged predators especially those with badges.

Juanito cast his countenance upon the heavens and realized that nature's daily slumber was about to gradually transform into birds chirping, woodpeckers pecking, and roadrunners running and scampering along their narrow trails then at a given moment, flying for short distances in explosive fashion like a line drive. The forest would soon be pulsating with life burst asunder from its innumerable permanent inhabitants from the animal world.

He nimbly made his way down from the upper heights of the cottonwood tree in which he had sought refuge the previous night from anything or anybody that might have wanted to jeopardize him in any way, form, or fashion. At about four meters above the ground, he abruptly halted his downward motion to tune in to everything that surrounded him and remained that way for at least a half hour. Perchance in that interim, he might hear something or, when it got lighter, see something that might possibly oblige him to replot his course to the coast. The sun's rays were now cleaving the horizon, separating darkness from light. Within a few minutes hence, Juanito was hearing cowbells, mooing, chickens clucking, ducks quaking, turkeys gobbling, and human speech. He continued his gradual downward spiral movement until his tire-tread-covered soles were standing on solid ground.

Still in the shadows and facing south, he observed several young Indigenous fishermen at the river's edge, about fifty meters away, stretching and yawning, about to begin their day on the river water where they would hopefully haul in an excellent catch using their nets. Behind them were several women and children (all early birds), carrying some baskets and bags containing breakfast, lunch, and snacks.

The women wore long dresses and shawls draped from their heads which the unmarried ones also managed to use as veils. Simple goat-hide sandals were the common footwear. Tehueco was a 100 percent Indigenous village originally founded by the Jesuits centuries before in their quest to Catholicize planet Earth. All its inhabitants spoke Spanish fluently, as a second language, and Mayo as a first language. Juanito remained in the shadows observing the Mayo women who were a decent stone's throw away. Once they had lovingly given their menfolk the prepared vittles, they would be munching on the rest of the day. Out in the water or on the river's edge, they returned to the kitchen to make corn tortillas—by hand! Furthermore, they would also be carrying out the daily domestic responsibilities as well as feeding the animals, milking those that needed to be milked, looking for/collecting eggs, and raking manure into small piles and then bigger piles, which would soon be spread out into their bean and cornfields. It had many uses.

CHAPTER 42

Corn Tortillas, Flour Tortillas, and the Law

The corn tortilla was and is the absolute cornerstone of the Mexican/Central American/Indigenous diet. It is the original tortilla. The flour tortilla is the new kid on the block. It is equally loved by millions of people in Mexico where it had its origin. Literally, just a few yards south of the west-flowing Fuerte River was a huge cornfield whose ears were ready to be harvested any day. Although Juanito was tempted to walk over to the fishermen who were still launching their pangas (skiffs) and offer them some money to take him several miles downstream, he wisely decided against it. Why? Because he couldn't be sure if there were any soldiers or policemen in the village ready to pounce on any stranger who happened to be ambling through.

Tehueco was a well-known crossing point for "medicinal plant" farmers (as well as a shortcut), so he wasn't willing to take any chances. Instead, as soon as the last of the beautiful Mayo women had headed back to their kitchens, and with the shadows still long, he ducked into the cornfield. From the vantage point of the cornfield, he was able to slowly encircle about half of Tehueco's perimeter, always staying low and remaining several meters from its edge. As usual, he made no noise and eventually found himself close to the village entrance, well hidden among the corn stalks. He was lucky to have been careful because there were state judicial police officers hidden in between several houses. Some of these houses were made of daub and pole, which was the traditional Mayo style. These traditional houses can withstand hurricanes and have been used since time immemorial. At any rate, Juanito had no choice but to remain hidden until the cops left. Since they hadn't nabbed anyone carrying dope or lots of cash, he felt they wouldn't be there that much longer. Fortunately, for Juanito, that was the case. By 10:00 a.m., the police were pulling out in their 4WDs, and that was that. He quietly moved back, always staying low, till he got to where he had first entered the cornfield.

Still camouflaged within the stalks, he just sat and listened for about fifteen minutes then decided it was safe to come out. He quickly disassembled his automatic weapon, a high-powered rifle, then inserted it, and all the *goma* plus most of the cash he had been carrying in his jacket into his backpack. Then he quietly dug a hole with his trusty machete, set his backpack within it, and covered it with a light layering of soil. On top of that, he placed fallen corn stalks, and soon it was completely camouflaged.

CHAPTER 43

Cornfields, Pangas, and Candy

Exiting the cornfield, he walked along the river's edge toward that point where the men had launched their *pangas*. He constantly had his eyes affixed on the village, always looking for any possible danger. When he got to the launching point, he stood there for a few seconds then strode into the village hoping to buy some breakfast to tide him over until evening. By that time, he hoped to be almost home.

Several small Mayo children came running up to him, laughing and jumping up and down. They wanted to know if he had any money for candy! Juanito just smiled and asked them where the store was. Pulling him by the arm, they were happy to oblige and took him directly to *Abarrotes Don Luis* (Don Luis' Groceries).

Don Luis was an elderly, full-blooded Mayo Indian (*Yoreme*), who, despite his countenance, was still physically quite active. He and his sons not only administered their large grocery store but also farmed a couple of hundred acres outside Tehueco and had a small herd of steers, dozens of goats, and so many chickens, turkeys, and ducks they had lost count. They had given up riding horses a long time ago and had opted instead for jeeps and cattle trucks. They were very well off. One of Don Luis's pet passions was fishing, both salt and fresh water.

As the children pulled Juanito into *Abarrotes Don Luis*, he became quite curious about the whole setting. *Might this guy be the one I am looking for?* he queried himself in the inner recesses of his mind. *If he owns or at least has access to a panga, I could make it worthwhile for him to just cross me over to the other side of the river then I'd be home free!*

"Don Luis! Don Luis!" good-naturedly called out the children. "We wanna buy some candy!" Don Luis came lumbering out to the counter from a back room with a big smile on his face. He happily greeted the children then courteously received Juanito with a nod and a hello then asked what he could do for him.

The children responded before Juanito could even muster up a word. "He wants to buy us some candy!"

At their young age, the children already knew that when any non-Mayos were present, they needed to speak in Spanish, not in *Cahita. Cahita*, their true language was/is an Indigenous tongue spoken by the Mayos and their first cousins to the North, the Yaquis. In fact, Cahita is the only Indigenous (Pacific) coastal language that the Spanish Crown couldn't exterminate despite well-organized efforts to eradicate it over the centuries. Everyone was speaking in Spanish for Juanito's sake. Don Luis confirmed with Juanito what he had been told by the Mayo children, then Juanito told Don Luis to give each child fifty pesos worth of candy and to ask each one precisely what kind they wanted. After parceling out the candy, Don Luis told the children to go out and play. He knew from the get-go that Juanito wasn't just there to buy candy.

CHAPTER 44

Don Luis, Weapons, and a Fast-Moving Current

"What can I really do for you, young man? I know you're not in Tehueco just to buy candy," he asserted, looking at Juanito straight in the eye.

"You've read me like a book, Don Luis, so I'll just cut to the chase. I need to cross the river as soon as possible, and I was hoping you could point me in the right direction. I'll pay well"

Don Luis sized Juanito up for several seconds then asked him how much he was willing to pay and where exactly did he want to be docked.

"Across would be just fine, but if I'm taken downriver a few hundred meters that would work too. Do you know someone?"

"Yes, sir! You are looking at him."

They spoke for a few minutes, then Juanito took him to where he had his weapon stashed. After looking it over, he nodded his head. He had accepted it as pay.

In thirty minutes, Don Luis had his panga in the water, and he was ready to start the motor and take off. Juanito had been waiting for him at the river's edge and got on board as soon as it was in the water. Don Luis carefully got on board, sat down, then told Juanito they were going to let the fast-moving current take them down the river a few kilometers to a beach where Juanito could get off.

Don Luis paddled out a few meters, then the current took over. Before long, Don Luis had the paddle in his hand once again and was deftly rowing toward the previously mentioned beach. With one final mighty stroke, the panga's bow was on the beach. Juanito quickly jumped off, thanking Don Luis, who in turn gave him several fat piping-hot burritos wrapped in a small towel along with some fiery chiltepin chiles and a small gourd full of cool well water. Now Juanito wouldn't have to stop along the way seeking food to satiate his hunger. Since it was the rainy season, there were many brooks and water holes available—more than enough to quench his thirst. Bidding Don Luis farewell, Juanito didn't waste any time and was soon quickly striding in a north-westerly direction toward his home in El Poblado 5, Sinaloa.

He was now carrying a much lighter load: the raw opium (la amapola), his .45 automatic, a big bowie knife, a razor-sharp hooked machete, a blanket, some toiletries, the burritos, and the gourd. With this light load, he was able to cut a quick path in his tire-tread sandals through the dense, thorn-infested brush. He only stopped walking when nature called. He even kept striding when he ate or drank water.

Along the way, he spotted more rabbits and other small critters than he could shake a stick at and even a few deer and some peccaries (a small but dangerous wild boar). When the sun set, he kept on truckin' oblivious to everything except his final goal: El Poblado 5. Now and then, he would even trot. After fifteen hours of military-like striding, and in the dead of night, he espied Federal Highway 15 which passed right in front of his community. In less than an hour, he was home. By that time, it had already dawned, and his wife and two children were on their feet as soon as he walked through the door. Showering him with kisses and hugs mixed with loving laughter, his wife was soon preparing him a breakfast to die for. Home at last!

Juanito planned to be back up in the mountains in a couple of weeks to finalize the growing season which meant selling all the marijuana and opium stashed in the cave. He was going to be in for the shock of his life when he got there. After that moment, he wouldn't be at peace until he had exacted retribution from Omar. That was still several years in the future.

CHAPTER 45

Final Chapter

Upon delivering the merchandise to the captain, Omar also explained to him how the four guys would be needing a ride down to Choix so they could catch a bus back to the coast. He also requested a helicopter ride for himself to the outskirts of Los Mochis since he *would be carrying all that money.* He had sold four of the five kilos of opium to the captain for a significant amount and intended to have the remaining kilo processed on the coast which would give him one hundred grams of pure black heroin known as Mexican Mud.

His aim was to conceal the heroin in a suitcase and then smuggle it to the US border on a bus. Before boarding the bus, he would have tightly enclosed it in plastic stretch wrap then stuffed it into a small plastic container that was full of raw sheep fat and then plugged it. Why raw sheep fat? Because raw sheep fat totally conceals, with zero secretion, the scent of heroin. This is a must because some of the checkpoints have trained *sniffer* K9s. Once on the border, he would then bootleg it over to the US in the dead of night through a place he had *hopped over* several times before, years ago, with others, looking for work in the States.

Once on the other side, he would stealthily creep through the brush for a couple of miles until he got to a highway where he and other undocumented persons, years ago, would be picked up on certain days and hours by human smugglers. The smugglers knew the border patrol's exact hours of operation and their desert beat. Once near the highway, he would ditch the heroin in some desert brush and then walk nearly twenty miles to a small town where he knew some people from Sinaloa. From there, on a given night, he would be dropped off near the stashed heroin, pluck it out of its hiding place, then cautiously hike another twenty miles to the same small town thus circumventing all highway checkpoints and easily avoiding all border patrol vehicle routes because he would have been apprised of their beat.

The border patrol had allegedly been using night-vision binoculars for decades to be able to capture more undocumented individuals attempting to cross over at night. This strategy has apparently met with little success because more people than ever are making the crossing without hindrance. Hmmm? A week later, Omar was in Chicago with the merchandise and a false green card.

He would remain there for the next three years dealing dope and working in a car wash, yes, a car wash! He sold the Mexican Mud strictly retail and had it cut several times to maximize his profit. With the dope money, he was able to buy a used Toyota Tacoma, which was still in almost mint condition and purchased a brand-new wardrobe. He had left $45,000 of the $50,000 with his parents under the strict agreement that they would deeply bury it somewhere on their acreage in $5,000 parcels. That meant one hole for each parcel and not touching them for at least a year because soon Juanito would be spying on them. Caution, strict ironclad caution, was the name of the game here.

Once they were finally able to begin using the ill-gotten cash, it would have to be in small increments. Plus, for obvious reasons, they would have no choice but to exchange the US dollars for pesos in a money exchange house from as far away as possible from Los Mochis. They would probably wind up taking the bus to Culiacan, the state capital, to effect said transactions because no one knew them there.

Eventually Omar would make his way back to Sinaloa, much to his chagrin, because Juanito would be waiting for him. Omar was quite cognizant of this but nonetheless was quite willing to take the chance because he needed to see his mom and dad. They weren't getting any younger, so it was well worth the risk—or so he thought. But, dear reader, that's a whole different story!

ABOUT THE AUTHOR

As a youngster and young adult, I, the author, spent a lot of time in Sinaloa, Mexico, with my grandfather. He lived way out in the country in a small village located in a farming community. At that juncture in time, many residents of the said community didn't have access to potable water or electricity. The closest phone was three miles away and paved roads were almost nonexistent. There were only two black-and-white television sets in the small community, and my grandpa owned one of them. This was circa 1969. The other one was owned by Machi, the local mom-and-pop grocery store owner.

Every Saturday night at eight, a three-hour boxing card was transmitted from the Arena Coliseo in Mexico City, and Machi's store would be packed with male boxing fans from all over the small village. The fans were comprised mostly of adults of all ages and a few adolescents. That was where I fit in. I was a teenager back then and over time would be one of the (young) adults.

By the time the first six-round bout was over, the small store would be teeming with tobacco smoke, and the entire front entrance would be wide open. Before the main event, there were a couple of more six-rounders, one or two eight-rounders, then the main event, a ten-rounder.

By the time the main event started, Machi would have sold all his soft drinks, his Mexican sweet bread, his candy bars, chips, and a bunch of sandwiches he would have made for the occasion. All his cigarettes would be gone too. Before the actual card kicked off and between rounds, the older adults would talk about current events, politics, the economy, philosophy, and other things. Sooner or later though, the conversation would revolve around the drug trade taking place in the high mountains. There were always a few men present who had firsthand experience in that illegal enterprise.

They would talk freely about their years of experience in that business because they were around family and old friends. Not only that, but they also had family and friends who worked in law enforcement and who would keep them apprised of any impending danger and such.

For years and years, I heard firsthand accounts from individuals who had worked in the high mountains growing opium poppies and marijuana. I heard those stories so many times they were etched into my memory. This book is squarely based on those many firsthand accounts. By the way, some of those men I never saw again because they were either killed or arrested in the high mountains. It's a dangerous business!

www.ingramcontent.com/pod-product-compliance
Lightning Source LLC
Chambersburg PA
CBHW021003180726
47993CB00017B/571